THE DEFI REVOLUTION

WHAT YOU NEED TO KNOW ABOUT HOW
DECENTRALIZED FINANCE AND BLOCKCHAIN
TECHNOLOGY ARE DISRUPTING THE WORLD, AND
HOW TO PROFIT

EUGENE MCKINNEY

D1264476

CONTENTS

INTRODUCTION

If someone asked you what sector grew the fastest during the 2020 coronavirus pandemic, what would you say? Stocks, consumer goods, toilet paper? It turns out that decentralized finance, which includes cryptocurrencies and blockchain technology, grew 2,000 percent in less than a year (Shapira, 2020).[1]

You've heard of crypto and blockchain, but you may not know exactly how they work. In this book, you'll discover all you need to know about decentralized finance (DeFi) and, more importantly, how to harness that kind of growth potential for your own use.

Do you have friends who talk about their cryptocurrency wallets all the time? It sounds interesting, but you're afraid to say anything that might demonstrate how little you know about it. You've probably heard that some well-known investors, hedge fund titans, and tech superstars such as Bill Gates have bought cryptocurrency.

You want to get in as soon as you can, knowing that as soon as more people understand the value of it that you can expect prices to rise. But you're not confident that you know enough about it to make a smart investment.

Terms such as *crypto, blockchain, DeFi* are so new that they seem overwhelming. It seems like the smart money is getting in and getting in fast. You don't want to lose all your money by getting into something you don't understand, but at the same time you'd like to make some money. If so many investors are buying in, what do they know that you don't?

Once you've learned the fundamentals of DeFi, you'll be able to decide for yourself what you want to invest in and how much you're comfortable buying. Reading this book provides you with the knowledge you need to take action and invest wisely. Instead of being confused by all the new technology, you'll have a grasp of what it is and how you can make money from it.

Best of all, you don't have to be Bill Gates or the founder of a billion-dollar hedge fund to profit from the world of DeFi. Only certain people who are accredited investors with a million dollars in security investments and incomes of at least a quarter of a million are permitted to buy into a hedge fund.

The whole point of blockchain and DeFi is to remove these types of gates and gatekeepers to the financial frontier. By removing the middlemen, or institutions like banks and hedge funds, the technology is open to anyone who has the knowledge and interest.

By picking up this book, you've shown that you have the interest. By the time you finish reading, you'll have the knowledge. First, you'll discover the basics of decentralized finance, and what that term really means. You'll understand why it's so important, and why it's becoming ever more popular.

Learning about the advantages of DeFi will show you why many investors believe it solves problems in the current financial landscape. You'll read about crypto that's pegged to a real-world asset and smart contracts that take the place of exchanges like the ones used to trade stocks.

Once you have the fundamentals of this new financial technology down, you'll be able to leverage it to make money. DeFi can help you save differently and borrow differently. Insurance can be used to make transactions even more secure.

As with everything in the world of finance, there is no free lunch. The technology does have downside risks that you need to be aware of and prepare for if you're going to invest. You'll also see how DeFi has the opportunity to make capital accessible to people all over the world, whether they're investors, entrepreneurs, or anything else.

Now that you know what I've written in the book, you might be asking yourself why you should listen to me specifically. You already know that the topic can be hard to understand and that you need an expert to help you decrypt the info on crypto. I've been deeply engaged in the DeFi space since 2014 as a tech professional and tech blogger.

I've been experimenting with blockchain technology the entire time, so I've actually gotten my hands dirty and seen what works and what doesn't. In addition, I actively educate others about the space through my blogging platform. In other words, I've been doing this for a while, relative to how long the tech's been available.

I believe DeFi has the potential to significantly disrupt the way money and finance works, and I'm committed to helping as many people as I can to learn about it and, better yet, make profit off it. Now is a great time for beginners to get started, which is why I've put together this guide with everything you need to know.

I'm passionate about introducing people to this new technology and helping them become experts themselves. To be honest, back in 2014 I was in your shoes: what is this stuff and what does it mean for me? Now I know and I'm sharing it with as many people as I can. Instead of teaching people one by one, the book allows me to get the message out to a much wider audience.

The longer you take to read the book and start taking action, the farther away your goal of profiting off DeFi will be. Why delay knowledge that can pump up your assets? Jump into the book and get started.

1

DEMYSTIFYING DECENTRALIZED FINANCE

B efore we begin on decentralized finance (DeFi), it might be helpful to take a (short) stroll down memory lane in terms of modern finance and how it works. The free market provides buyers and sellers with the opportunity to exchange with each other, and right now most of those transactions occur through intermediaries.

The 21st Century world of financial intermediaries

If you want to buy shares of a company stock, for example, you use a stock exchange to find a seller who provides the shares at a price you're willing to pay. Most likely, you're making the transaction from an online trading platform and paying a commission to do so. Your payment compensates the platform for its role in the purchase you're making. Most transactions involving money use intermediaries or middlemen, who take some payment for their involvement.

The electronic trading platforms are, believe it or not, a step above the 20th Century way of investing in the market. Before the Internet, you would have to have a broker who you would call to do the trade. Those commissions were much higher even than the ones you pay to modern trading platforms.

Intermediaries make transactions potentially more expensive than they need to be. It also introduces gatekeepers to some of the markets, so if you want to buy into a hedge fund or private equity firm you need to have a certain net worth and income to do so.

In the type of centralized financial world that we mostly have now, central banks are key to the economies of major developed countries. Here, in the US, the central bank is known as the Federal Reserve (the Fed). It can raise or lower interest rates to pump more money in, or take money out which it typically does if inflation is running high - more about this later in the book.

If the Fed raises the interest rate at which it lends money, then all the lending institutions that must raise their interest rates too, otherwise they'll be unprofitable. The banks act as intermediaries for the loans.

Suppose you want to take out a mortgage so you can buy a house. Once the Fed raises rates (or "tightens" them), the bank will raise the interest rate for mortgages, too and take a cut for making the loan.

Intermediaries employ a lot of people, which means they need to make a certain amount of profit to stay in business. Typically, the person who sells you a mortgage is not the same person who *underwrites* it (decides how risky you are and how high your interest rate should be), even though they work for the same institution.

Each lender has its own policies about writing loans, such as what credit score a borrower needs to have, and other conditions of the loan. You might qualify for a mortgage at one bank and not at another, or face a higher interest rate at one company compared to the other one just down the road. In addition, you'll pay a variety of fees associated with the mortgage loan (or any loan).

At this point you might be asking yourself, why do we need intermediaries in the first place, since they cost so much? When money is involved, so is trust. Intermediaries are neutral third-parties in a transaction that don't have a stake in the outcome.

In the old days, companies would issue actual share certificates for their stock. Suppose you agreed with a seller that you'd buy 10 shares of, say, American Amalgamated Agency Association (AAAA).

What happens if you send the seller your money and they never send you the certificates? You can't prove that you own the shares, and so you can't profit by selling them once the share price reaches a new high. Conversely, suppose the seller sent you the certificates and you never ponied up the money. Now the seller has no shares, so they can't sell to someone who will pay them, and no money.

The easiest way to solve this particular kind of problem is an intermediary, in this case, a clearing house. The seller sends the certificates to the clearing house, which keeps track of the owner of the shares, for a fee. Then, when you buy them, the clearing house notes that you're the new owner of those shares. You pay them the seller's price, plus a fee for the clearing house. After the house takes its cut, it passes the remainder to the seller.

Companies don't issue stock certificates anymore and the records are all electronic, but the steps are the same. The middleman or intermediary takes their cut either way.

Introducing blockchain technology

Humans didn't always need intermediaries and middlemen. In the early days of human history, people lived in small tribes or groups. Everyone knew everyone. If you agreed to trade something with someone in your village, and you didn't hold up your end of the trade, you could expect an unfriendly visit from the person you cheated. Potentially that person might show up with a group of large, hostile friends of theirs, as well.

The system worked based on trust, because there were consequences to not holding up your end of the bargain. It was also pretty transparent. Whoever needed to know about the transaction would be told. In a small village, as those of you who live in small towns know, there aren't a whole lot of secrets.

Blockchain, also known as Distributed Ledger Technology, is a tech-based type of ledger that replicates this transparency and trust without bringing in middlemen and their associated expenses. It's a little bit like the Google Doc I'm writing this book on, as well. Docs are shared with a group of people (in my case, my editor also has access), which is the same as being distributed. My editor isn't working on a copy of the document but on the actual doc, and any modifications that either of us make are immediately available to the other, so it's completely transparent.

I know and trust my editor, but with blockchain you don't have to know or trust any of the other distributees to trust that the record is correct. It's all done through technology.

There are three major aspects to blockchain technology.

1. Each chain, as the name suggests, is made up of blocks.

A block contains a number of transactions and is encrypted and time-stamped. Every block in the chain references the previous block.

A major benefit of developing a chain in this way is that it's immediately clear when a block has been tampered with. In order to commit fraud, someone would have to alter all the blocks in the chain, for every version of the chain. Not only is this an extreme amount of work, it's also very hard work (which we'll get into below).

Due to this kind of transparency and difficulty in changing the chain, participants can trust the data even when they don't know the identity of the other participants.

Each participant in the chain has their own identification that shows all their transactions. That maintains the transparency of the chain, and allows trust and verification to take place for secure transactions. The ID isn't based on real-world data, so you still have privacy even though the transactions are transparent to all.

2. Miners are required for new blocks on the chain.

They are integral to the process of preventing fraud. In real life, have you ever gone to a store with a large denomination like a $100 bill and tried to purchase a small item? You'll notice the cashier hold the bill up to the light, or maybe even check it on a special machine. They're trying to determine if the bill is real, or whether you're trying to pass off a counterfeit and get real bills in exchange.

For money in the physical world, there are a variety of ways to check for counterfeiting. It's harder online where perfect copies can be made and there's no way to verify whether what you have is the original or not.

Miners in the blockchain are the ones that handle the verification. On their computers they "listen" for transactions and create a list of valid transactions. They check for two things on a request: one, that the digital signature matches with the transaction, and two, that the transaction hasn't already happened, which they verify on the blockchain. Each user has their own copy of the blockchain.

For example, suppose that you want to buy something that costs seven Bitcoin. Previously you received three from user A and four from user B. On your request, you specify the three from A and four from B. Miners verify that your digital signature matches what A and B sent, and also that you have not previously spent your seven Bitcoin.

If the miner verifies that the request is legit, they add it to their list. Every ten minutes a miner is chosen to add their list, or block, to the blockchain, which keeps the chain up to date.

In order to prevent miners from committing fraud, they compete by guessing what the right number (hash) is, which requires dedicated software. The more powerful a computer that the miner has, the more tries they can make at a hash that results in "winning" the block.

Unlike current platforms and databases where gaining entry to one user (through hacking, bad actors, or whatever) gives access to all the data, someone mining the blockchain needs to spend a lot of time and energy on it.

3. Nodes connected to the chain maintain the integrity of it.

The ledger is decentralized, so there's no one company, organization, or nation that controls any specific blockchain. Any electronic device can function as a node and keep the network operating. Typically a node is a computer, laptop, or even a server.

The nodes each have their own copy of the blockchain and must approve (via algorithm) any mining to update the blockchain. A full node contains a copy of the entire blockchain.

Once a miner has verified a block, it sends the information to all the nodes on the chain. They check that the block is legitimate, and if so, add it on top of the other blocks on its copy of the chain.

While miners are nodes themselves, because they need a full node to verify transactions, not all nodes are miners. Some nodes may contain the blockchain but do no mining themselves. Not all nodes are online all the time. After they've been offline, they need to download all the blocks that have appeared since they were last online. That's known as syncing to the blockchain.

Developers are able to create computer programs that talk to each other on the blockchain. Automating processes allows blockchain technology to expand into a variety of industries, and removes humans and their habits of making mistakes from the operations.

The programming instructions can tell the chain how to perform whatever functionality is required. Everything from musical intellectual property to healthcare records to finance can be executed securely (Builtin, n.d.).[1] Currently, many different industries are learning how to work with and take advantage of blockchain technology.

These programs are known in the DeFi world as *smart contracts*, and they execute automatically when specific conditions are met on the blockchain. Programs may also be known as *dapps* (decentralized apps) because they're built on top of decentralized tech. By contrast, apps that you're familiar with from Google Play or Apple Store are mostly centralized, owned by a developer or company.

Basics of cryptocurrency

Before there were smart contracts, blockchain tech was used to send and receive *crypto*. This is digital money that can be used to buy and sell online, or traded for profit. Many companies issue their own crypto in the form of tokens that you can swap for their products and services.

There are a ton of different cryptocurrencies currently available. As of February 2021, there were about 7,300 different "coins" and a total value of about $1.6 trillion (Royal et al, 2021).[2] You might be familiar with the o.g. token, Bitcoin. New crypto appears regularly through initial coin offerings (ICOs).

Unlike currencies such as the dollar, euro, and British pound, there are no central banks that affect the performance of crypto. A country or entity's central bank may have a mandate (such as fighting inflation) that affects the value of the currency but has nothing to do with free market forces. Some users like crypto for this reason.

Like all currencies, crypto doesn't generate any cash flow. At the moment, investing in crypto is mainly for speculators who want to sell at a profit. For currencies to be widely accepted, they must have some stability so people can figure out what a fair price is for any given product or service. It's hard to do that when the value of the currency fluctuates wildly, which has been true of crypto since the beginning.

People who want to get involved in crypto need an online wallet to hold their investments. An unfortunate number of investors have lost significant amounts of cryptocurrency because they forgot the password to their digital wallet! That number could be as high as 20 percent of total value for Bitcoin (Campbell, 2021).[3] The digital wallet is similar to a bank account online, except much harder to hack - or get into if you forget your password.

Decentralized finance

Cryptocurrencies, dapps, and blockchain are all part of DeFi, or the push to make every financial service that you can think of global, decentralized, and transparent. You can think of it as financial applications created on top of the blockchain.

Savings, borrowing money, insurance, and trading can all be done without the intermediaries and institutions that are integral to today's world of money. Instead of running financial checking and savings accounts through the banks, anyone in the world can access money as long as they have a phone and Internet connection.

In the next chapter, we'll delve into the DeFi advantages more specifically. They result from the differences between decentralized finance (sometimes called open finance) and the centralized systems that are currently in use.

Decentralized rules and policies

There's no central bank dictating limits on a cryptocurrency, or banking institution making the rules about who has access to their funds. Instead, smart contracts or computer code maintain the rules. In addition to cutting out the intermediary cost, allowing smart contracts means that the tech can basically run itself without a lot of human interference.

In practical terms, developers need to maintain their dapps with bug fixes or upgrades, just like other software programmers.

There's no reason, though, that a transaction must go through multiple levels of human approval.

Global functionality

Most (current) applications and financial systems software are designed for the major currencies in play and their organizations, namely the Euro, US dollar, British pound, and Chinese renminbi/yuan.

Dapps, by contrast, are designed to work globally. Cryptocurrencies are in global use around the world. Bitcoin is Bitcoin whether you're located in the US, Zimbabwe, or Uruguay.

No gatekeepers

Dapps are "permissionless" by design, so that anyone can use and create them. No forms to fill out, online or off. All you need is your online wallet. There are no "accredited investors" when it comes to crypto or any other DeFi possibility.

Can build on each other

Because the programs are all open-source, developers can mix and match what's already out there to create a new product. There's no intellectual property protection to navigate if you want to use something that DeFi has already created.

Independent

In the traditional world, there's what's known as "open banking." Third-party financial software providers can get access to data held at financial institutions such as banks through APIs or application programming interfaces. This allows companies to integrate data held in different places to provide new solutions for their customers.

For example, small business bookkeeping software can hook into the owner's business banking and credit card accounts as well as payment processors. That way the data on what's been bought and sold flows automatically into the bookkeeping system, without the owner having to manually enter receipts.

Open banking is definitely an upgrade to more manual systems and permits new software products within the traditional system. Open finance (DeFi) is completely independent of this traditional infrastructure and allows for entirely new potential financial instruments.

Why is DeFi growing in popularity?

Before we had fast internet, decentralized finance wasn't even possible. Gains in technology are one of the factors driving the adoption of DeFi. As more applications are developed and the use cases proliferate, the more influential people begin to adopt it.

Yet in addition to providing for the wealthy and influential, DeFi enables those who haven't had much access to capital to get money as well. People who haven't previously been served by traditional finance are able to get in the game, and this is a huge market for a variety of reasons we'll get into in the next chapter.

At the beginning, cryptocurrencies had no collateral behind them. In this they're very similar to the US dollar once it was removed from the gold standard, and the euro and British pound, which all "float." As crypto has matured, however, *stablecoins* have developed which are pegged to some reference, often collateral such as the US dollar.

In theory, stablecoins shouldn't fluctuate as wildly as other crypto does. In practice there's more volatility than most investors want, though that may be due to how young the technology is.

Lending platforms have also started to grow through DeFi, and they provide a measure of privacy that traditional lending doesn't. If you want to borrow money from a traditional lender, they'll scrape up your credit score and history, maybe look at your tax returns depending on the type of loan, and ask for an income history.

If you borrow using DeFi, on the other hand, all you need is collateral, typically some form of crypto. It doesn't matter what your credit score is or how much you make in income or who you are as long as you have the collateral. Most DeFi runs on the Ethereum platform which allows for smart contracts (Bitcoin does not), so usually the collateral is in the form of ether, which is the platform's cryptocurrency.

Chapter Summary

Decentralized finance is designed to address some of the important shortcomings of our current, traditional financial system.

- Intermediaries are the backbone of the current system, and they provide trust in the system.
- Blockchain technology uses computers and math to make a secure system that anyone can audit, verify, and trust.
- Cryptocurrency (such as Bitcoin and ether) were some of the first blockchain applications.
- DeFi uses the principles of blockchain to create a new financial system that is open to all, more transparent, and permissionless.
- Open finance has grown in popularity as new uses are discovered and spread throughout the global ecosystem.

2

THE ADVANTAGES OF DEFI

I n the last chapter, you discovered the ways in which DeFi is different from the traditional financial system that's currently in use. Due to the security of blockchain technology, it makes a lot of sense to move sensitive transactions onto a platform that's much harder to hack than current financial institutions are. In addition, there are some distinct advantages that decentralized finance brings to the world of money that more and more people all over the globe are beginning to use to their benefit.

Transparency

Just to be clear, transparency doesn't mean that everyone else on the blockchain can see what you personally have done or invested in. Users are identified by a string of alphanumeric characters that can't be traced to you in real life. Even if you and

I are on the same blockchain, you can't see that I, Eugene McKinney, have bought so much Ether or used Bitcoin to invest in online real estate. You can see that so much Ether was purchased by a user, but you can't tell who the user is.

It's a bit like watching the stock ticker, because share prices are updated to reflect the latest trading activity. There is an important difference, however: on the ticker, you can't see who bought stock in AAAA. You'll just see the price and number of shares traded move. On the blockchain, you can see all the transactions occurring as soon as mined blocks are authenticated and verified.

Why is that such an advantage? For one thing, it cuts down significantly on fraud. This is excellent for financial operations because it makes audits much easier. No such thing as the keeping of two ledgers (one real and one for busybodies), because everyone has all the same access to the information. Every transaction can be traced - no shuffling around between business entities and conveniently "losing" a little here and a little there.

Because all the transactions are immutable and can't be removed from the chain, you can see the entire history. This also cuts down on fraud, because the transactions can't be amended to show something else. We'll talk more about the advantages of decentralization in a later section but it, plus the transparency factor, prevents any one single entity from controlling the chain and trying to manipulate data in its favor.

It can also revolutionize gaming and predictive markets where users bet on anything from who will win the next large sports contest to the next large national election to all kinds of other gambles. Having "provable fairness" might induce more players to the games, because they wouldn't be concerned about having the deck stacked against them (HBUS, 2018).[1] When it comes to casinos, online or off, the house is always in favor but players can check to make sure that their results are fair and real.

Interoperability

Like a pile of Legos, developers can take dapps that have already been made and add them to new apps or change apps to their liking. In this way, users have a more seamless experience moving money around or performing transactions for a variety of needs. It creates the opportunity to develop completely new applications on the blockchain.

Another facet of interoperability has yet to be realized, which is to be able to move from one blockchain technology to another. For example, suppose you have Bitcoin and want to buy something on the Ethereum network. Currently developers are working on how to standardize some of the protocols so that it doesn't matter what platform you use, you can move about in the DeFi world.

Another potential solution is to hook them together via APIs, as traditional finance does now. There are some authenticity concerns with this method, however, not to mention that it requires the platforms to connect one-to-one rather than forming a network or consortium.

Independence from traditional financial structures

Many modern money applications are strictly regulated, especially in the US and Europe. At first, plenty of early adopters latched onto crypto as a way to escape financial scrutiny and to make purchases on the "dark web." Sites on the dark (or "deep") web are typically encrypted in a way that they don't appear on traditional search engines.

Many of these sites are perfectly legal, such as private files hosted on secure document sites like Dropbox and its competitors. It's also used by political dissidents from authoritarian countries that restrict such activities to prevent them from being tossed in jail.

There is, however, illegal activity on the dark web, such as the trading of stolen credit card numbers and buying drugs in areas where they're not legalized. You can see why someone who's dealing with illicit affairs would prefer to keep their search activity anonymous, and pay for their products and services in a way that's untraceable to all but the most sophisticated cybersecurity teams.

Having said all that, being independent from traditional finance is of huge benefit to many people around the world who don't have access to capital, typically those living in less developed countries or who are below the poverty line in developed ones.

As an example, in order to trade stocks in the US, you typically need a checking account from an accredited financial institution like a bank, credit union, or brokerage firm to begin with. The usual way to open up such an account is to go there in person, show your government-issued ID and proof of residence and fill out a number of documents. Technology has made it possible for people to fill out documents online, but it's also often difficult to do over mobile technology so it's best to have an Internet connection.

Many banks charge fees just to have the account open, unless you can set up a direct deposit into the account on a regular basis. In other words, just to open an account, you need an address where you can prove that you're living (with a utility bill in your name or some such), a tablet or laptop and stable internet connection or bank branch in your location.

You also need either enough money to handle the regular fees, or have a job in which you're paid via direct deposit, or a job where you have regular paychecks that don't all go towards your basic needs such as housing and food. If you don't have direct deposit from your employer, it helps to have just one job that gives you the flexibility to go to the bank and deposit the money when you need to.

In the US, residents of poorer neighborhoods are typically "unbanked" because there are too many barriers to opening a bank account. Many financial institutions don't have a presence in these neighborhoods at all.

Workers often go to the payday loan place to cash their checks, which takes a huge bite out of their money to begin with. Payday loan shops serve these customers by being available early in the morning and late at night, and not requiring much in the way of Internet connections or documents to hand over the cash they need to pay bills.

For similar reasons, many people in developing countries don't have access to traditional money structures either. The banks don't exist at all, or they're known to be untrustworthy. Internet connection may be spotty or nonexistent, depending on location.

When just trying to access money from your paycheck is so difficult, imagine how hard everything else is as well. In the US, the wealth of the middle class tends to be concentrated in their homes as assets. Depending on where you live, it might be impossible to save up enough money to buy a house outright, so you need to take out a mortgage.

If you've ever done that, you know how much of a nightmare it is. You need a solid credit score, which means you need to have credit in the first place. You'll show the bank your tax returns, pay stubs to verify your income, and sign off on pages and pages of documents. If you're counting any other income (such as spousal support) you have to document that as well. The house itself must meet certain standards for conventional loans.

Not only are you faced with paying interest for years on end, you also have to come up with a down payment and more fees for a single transaction than you've ever seen in your life. The bank usually makes you pay for the loan process itself (loan origination fee). You'll also pay for the title search and documentation, your real estate agent (if you have one), the escrow agent who holds your money, etc., etc.

All that documentation can be very hard for the unbanked to come by, even if they've regularly been making rent payments. People without a credit card might find it hard to find an affordable loan, because they don't have credit in their name and therefore no credit history. Again, this can be true even if they pay their other bills on time.

Yet there are many reasons why the unbanked should have the same access to capital as middle class people in developed countries with stable jobs and internet access. There are plenty of budding entrepreneurs in undeveloped countries and unbanked locations who could use a small start-up loan. Anyone can learn how to trade stocks, so why should someone be held back because they don't have a checking account?

Blockchain technology and crypto provide a path to money that people need without demanding the same infrastructure. With a little knowledge, a mobile phone and an online wallet, which most people across the globe do have access to, anyone can engage in DeFi and get the banking, loans, and other financial products they need. No need to visit anyone or line up reams of documents or prove that they live where they claim to live.

Low service costs

In addition to not needing the same expensive infrastructure, DeFi provides more people with access to capital without having to pay all the fees that go along with the entities inside that infrastructure. Even a basic checking account often comes with a fee to open it up, a monthly fee to keep it going, a fee to issue the debit card, a fee for printing checks, and a fee for overdrawing your account (pulling out more money than is actually in the account.) You'll have to pay if you take money out of a different bank's ATM: both your own bank and the other charge a fee.

If you're interested in trading securities or purchasing investments, there's a fee for opening up your brokerage account and various other fees. If one of your accounts is a retirement account (such as an IRA here in the US), expect to pay an additional fee for its administration too. Any type of loan comes with fees, plus the interest you're expected to pay on the principal (original amount) of the loan itself.

Each time your transaction passes through someone's hands in traditional finance, your cost of transaction increases in terms of both money and time. Middlemen must be paid!

When you want to take out a loan to buy a house, you'll talk to a loan officer, who probably has to pass your documentation on to their manager to sign off on it. Then it goes to the underwriter, who can take weeks or months to determine how much of a credit risk you are and what interest rate you should be charged. They'll likely need to send that to their department manager for approval before they contact you. That's at least four different touches on your loan, and all four pairs of hands need to be paid.

Removing intermediaries not only simplifies access to capital, but makes it cheaper, too. Having dapps that process information instead of people results in getting your money faster. Transparent rules and policies mean that you don't show up at your bank with a fistful of documents, only to find out that you're missing a key piece of information. Instead, you know what's necessary ahead of time. You can also see that it's a fair process because it's so transparent.

Global solutions

There's no real reason other than current infrastructure that people should only access capital from the country that they live in, or buy things from the country (or region) that they live in. Wealthy people can easily buy whatever they want across the world, and hire someone to do all the tedious work to make that possible. The rest of us don't live in that reality.

Most of us have difficulty buying products and services in other countries (unless we're using a global purchasing site, and even sometimes that throws a wrench in the process). If you live in the US, Eurozone, or UK, the currency exchange usually isn't much of a problem. If you live elsewhere, or want to buy something elsewhere, strap in for the ride!

The US and most other developed countries use *fiat currency.* That means that there's no collateral backing the money; it has no intrinsic value. Up until the 1970s, the US dollar was backed by gold, but America went off the gold standard during that decade. The value of gold fluctuates mightily, so going back to the gold standard won't make the dollar or any other currency more stable.

Fiat money gives the Fed more leniency when it comes to controlling inflation (which was a massive problem in the 20th Century but not so much in the 21st, yet.) The Fed can affect the supply and demand for the dollar, which means it has more weapons against inflation.

The exchange rates between fiat currencies float according to supply and demand. When you can buy more British pounds with a US dollar, Americans can buy more things from the UK and take trips over there. By contrast, when you buy more dollars with a British pound, the UK will import more from the US, so American companies benefit.

Supply and demand ebb and flow due to a variety of factors, but one of them is certainly what the global reserve currency is. The Bretton Woods agreement after WWII established the US dollar as the world's reserve currency (Amadeo 2020).[2]

Another method of establishing a national currency is to *peg* it to another country's currency. Nations that use a dollar peg keep their currency at a fixed exchange rate to the US dollar. While most nations that peg to another currency use the dollar, the second most popular type is a euro peg. Usually, a country with a dollar peg needs to have plenty of dollars on hand, so they tend to export a lot of their trade to the US. Similarly for euro pegs where the nation exports mainly to the Eurozone.

Because the dollar and euro float, it's hard to keep the pegs exact. Many countries use a price range instead. China pegs to a range for the US dollar and tries to keep its currency low, which makes their exports attractive to the US market.

Therefore, when you want to purchase something in a different country, you need to take the exchange rate into account. Not only that, but you'll likely need the local currency to effect the transaction. If you're an American who wants to buy a place in Italy for your retirement, you'll need to come up with the amount necessary in euros.

The dollar is (usually) not worth the same amount in Britain as it is in Italy, because the pound/dollar exchange rate is completely different from the euro/dollar rate, and those are both different from the pound/euro rate as well.

Even though that seems hard enough, those three are highly traded currencies so the exchange rate is pretty reasonable. Now imagine that you live in an undeveloped country and your currency is thinly traded (there's not much demand for it). If you want to exchange for another currency, the price will be higher because the demand is low.

Seems expensive, right? Don't forget that every time you exchange the currency, you have to pay the intermediary who does the exchange for you separately! You can see why a global currency or global coin is so attractive: a crypto token (such as Bitcoin) is worth the same in Italy as it is in Zimbabwe as it is in the US, no matter what each country's currencies or economies are doing.

Customizable user experience

When you're in the traditional financial system, you deal with whatever software that particular institution has chosen to use. If your banking interface is hard to understand and use, that's just too bad - your life is harder than it needs to be through no fault of your own.

However, in DeFi, if you don't like the interface on a dapp, you can build your own or use one that someone else has already developed. Smart contracts are open interfaces and anyone can build on them (see also interoperability). If you want to make your life easier by using applications that make intuitive sense to you, DeFi will let you do it.

Of course, it helps if you have some tech knowledge! Or a techie friend who can be enlisted in your quest. You'll be able to browse dapps through your mobile wallet, so you might also find something you like elsewhere and use that instead. As more and more users come to DeFi, designers are beginning to focus on ease of use and intuitiveness in their apps.

Technology does tend to expect that the early adopters have some knowledge. As applications and systems become more mainstream and more non-techies need to use it, the apps become much friendlier to all users.

Chapter Summary

Decentralized Finance provides a number of advantages compared to the traditional financial models currently in use. Blockchain and crypto open up capital to underserved populations who previously didn't have much access.

- Transparency helps prevent fraud and promote trust in the blockchain.
- Being independent of the traditional system allows many more people to enter the world of finance.
- Expenses are usually lower than what's found in the modern banking system.
- Since blockchain technology is global, currency issues are sidelined.
- Users can customize DeFi for their personal use.

3

DECENTRALIZED INFRASTRUCTURE AND SMART CONTRACTS

One of the major innovations in decentralized finance is the ability to create *smart contracts*. Instead of going through lawyers to devise and implement contracts, blockchain allows computers to do it automatically. Having the code responsible for specifying who does what reduces a lot of friction in transactions, which results in - you guessed it - lower costs.

Blockchain platforms

Bitcoin erupted onto the scene in 2009. More than a decade later, there are more software platforms that have emerged and compete with one another. Each supports different computer programming languages. Below are some of the largest, but this is by no means a complete list. The existence of all these platforms creates one of the problems with blockchain technology, which is that there's no agreed-upon protocol for different platforms to "talk" to one another. Someone using IBM blockchain can't access Bitcoin.

IBM has its own platform, IBM Blockchain, and a business unit dedicated to blockchain applications and technologies. Their permissioning is different and attracts other large companies. Languages are mostly Go and Java.

Multichain is open source, and helps different enterprises work together. Languages include Python, C and C++, and Javascript. Ripple, created in 2012, is known for speed and efficiency. It's used in finance, helping to connect banks, exchanges, and payments.

Ethereum, founded in 2014, is the backbone for decentralized finance. It pioneered the use of smart contracts. It's very active and open source, which allows it to serve as the foundation for more dapps. A variety of program languages are usable on Ethereum, including C++ and Python. Decentralized finance is always open - no waiting for 9 am US Eastern time for the New York exchange to start trading.

Ethereum and DeFi

While Bitcoin is the largest blockchain platform in terms of market capitalization (*market cap*), Ethereum is the second largest and the most active. It's similar to Bitcoin in terms of access for everyone and having rules that don't change in midstream. Countries can print their own money and devalue their currency for strategic reasons, but that's not possible on blockchain. Some Argentinians have used blockchain to escape the inflation plaguing their country.

The reason that Ethereum is used for decentralized finance is that it goes beyond a cryptocurrency, though ETH (ether) tokens are also widely used. It makes digital funds programmable, which is the basis for smart contracts. Unlike Bitcoin, you can borrow or lend money on Ethereum, schedule payments, invest in certain types of mutual funds, and more.

Being able to borrow on the blockchain means that you have access to credit without selling your tokens, which would be a taxable event. As noted earlier in the book, these loans take place without all the invasive data-gathering that the traditional finance system requires.

At the moment, techie types have access to *flash loans*, which could spread to the larger user base as blockchain becomes more mainstream. With these loans, the loan amount must be paid back in the same transaction. If it isn't, the transaction simply fails. Liquidity pools are available and funds that aren't in use can be diverted for the transaction and then replaced.

Sound impossible? A simple example would be if you saw an asset trading at $1 on one exchange and $1.10 on another. With a flash loan, you'd borrow the asset from the first exchange and then sell it on the second. The sale proceeds would pay back your loan, and the rest (minus a transaction fee) is profit to you.

If you weren't able to buy enough on the second exchange to pay back the loan, the transaction would simply fail as if the loan never happened.

As you can see, while some of the Ethereum dapps mimic traditional finance models, others truly take advantage of the blockchain to innovate. For example, you can stream payments and pay people's salaries by the second, so they don't have to wait two weeks until their next paycheck. Or you can rent items such as storage lockers and bikes by the second.

Ether is the native cryptocurrency on Ethereum, but all kinds of tokens are allowable. Decentralized exchanges allow users to trade tokens at any time of day or night. It's also a great place for crowdfunding, because everyone can see how the money is used for a particular project.

In fact, there's a new model of fundraising that's opened up with Ethereum: *quadratic funding*. It provides money to the projects that will provide benefit to the most people. First, a matching pool of funds is donated, and then public funding starts.

People can donate to a project to show that they support it. After the round is over, the matching pool is distributed such that the project with the most unique requests gets the most funding. In other words, if one project has 1,000 donors who each contributed $1 and another has one donor of $1,000, the first project will get more money (depending on the pool). It has more unique donors, and thus stands to benefit more people.

All of these activities are available to anyone in the world as long as they have an online wallet and internet access.

Smart contracts

These are Ethereum accounts that can hold money and send it out or refund it based on the conditions programmed into the contract. You could have a smart contract that puts a certain amount of money into your child's wallet each month while they're away at college. No additional distributees can be added in since blocks are so difficult to tamper with. Banks can get hacked, but your kid's money is safe. At least until they hit the ATM, anyway.

Your child doesn't have to wait until your check "clears" to access the money, which can take days depending on the traditional bank. On the blockchain, as soon as it's executed, the funds are in their wallet. There's no human intervention required to make it happen, nor can a bank employee being away on vacation affect the deposit.

Because the contracts are open source, they can be audited and viewed so bad contracts are spotted quickly. Remember, the accounts are pseudonymous, so no one knows that it's you sending money to your kid. Miners and nodes only see transactions between two accounts.

As long as the parameters specified in the code of the contract are met, the transaction will be executed. It's common to require a fee for performing the transaction. On Ethereum the transaction fees are paid in ether tokens, which is commonly referred to as "gas" (Levi et al, 2018).[1] At the moment most of the smart contracts are relatively simple in terms of the number of steps the logic of the code asks for. The more complexity, the more "gas" is needed to make it happen.

Technology is great... when it works

Decentralized finance does share a characteristic with traditional finance: there is no free lunch. There are always trade offs. DeFi isn't a magic bullet that fixes all the problems with conventional finance. While it's true that computer code can execute flawlessly over and over again when it's written correctly, the fact that it's written by humans means there's still plenty of room for error.

Developers still have to issue bug fixes for their dapps, just as they do for other applications. Back in the 1980s, programmers were trained to remember GIGO: Garbage In, Garbage Out. It's still true whether the code is written on the blockchain or not.

Another issue with smart contracts is that most of them are not particularly legible to non-programmers. Many people get the help of a trained lawyer when they're dealing with a complicated contract (such as a mortgage loan, house purchase, even an agent's agreement) to get the "legalese" translated into ordinary English.

However, even non-lawyers can usually understand very simple contracts, like the one you might sign to set up an automatic distribution from one bank account to another. Even simple smart contracts aren't readily accessible to non-tech people. Anyone entering into a smart contract now either needs to have their own expertise or to hire a programmer to explain the contract to them.

Over time, it's likely that the smart contracts will be easier to read so you don't have to have a programming expert by your side, but we're not quite there yet.

Many smart contracts require input from entities that are not on the blockchain. The blockchain can't pull this information from *off-chain* resources. The data has to be pushed to it, which can cause mismatches between nodes.

Suppose that a crop insurance smart contract pays the owner a certain amount any time the temperature drops below freezing (32 degrees Fahrenheit). As anyone who lives in the contiguous 48 knows, temperatures can fluctuate wildly minute to minute. Nodes may receive the information at different times, which could cause one node to reject the block because it received the temperature as 33 degrees instead.

One solution that's been proposed for this type of problem is a predefined, third-party *oracle* that pulls the relevant information and pushes it to the nodes at certain times. While it's certainly a workable solution, it introduces an intermediary into the equation, which is exactly what the blockchain is designed to prevent.

The oracle may also be a point of failure for the whole system. It might not push the information to the blockchain when necessary, provide data that's wrong, or even go out of business. An oracle could be hacked, which could compromise the security of the whole blockchain.

Chapter Summary

Although there are multiple blockchain platforms, Ethereum is the one most used for decentralized finance.

- In addition to Bitcoin and Ethereum, there are blockchain platforms, such as IBM Blockchain and Multichain, that accept a variety of computer programming languages.
- Ethereum operates not only with cryptocurrency, it provides the ability to send and refund money in addition to holding it.
- Smart contracts that are executed by computer code are the basis for Ethereum and DeFi.
- Issues still remain with buggy computer code and off-chain resources that affect smart contracts.

4

DECENTRALIZED (STABLE) MONEY

An important component of any financial system is the stability of the money used in transactions. It's hard to determine a price when monetary units fluctuate wildly, for a wide range of values. In order for the model to be sustainable, pricing needs to be dependable. Currently, many of the cryptocurrencies currently in use are subject to significant volatility in their value. How can DeFi be used on a wide scale when coins (tokens) vary so much in price? One word: stablecoin.

Compare crypto constancy

How much do bananas cost where you live? There are some fluctuations due to supply chain disruptions or if some kind of exotic insect starts threatening banana crops, but usually the bananas themselves are pretty stable when it comes to price.

Suppose a banana sells for $1.00 normally, plus or minus a few cents. Because the value of the US dollar is reasonably stable (though certainly it fluctuates a bit relative to other currencies), most of the time when you go to the grocery store your price ranges from, say, $1.95 to $2.05.

Now imagine that every time you go to the grocery store, you have no idea what the price will be. One week you pay $1, and the next week it's $0.68, a drop of 32 percent. The week after the price increases to $3 - over 300 percent. Maybe that doesn't seem like such a big deal, so let's raise the stakes a little bit.

Maybe every month your cable bill is $100. Until the cable company raises your rates again in another six months to a year, your $100 payment is pretty stable. What if one month later the price drops (without warning) to $68 instead? Awesome! Then the next month, it increases over 300 percent to $300 without any warning.

How do you maintain your budget when prices swing so wildly? When your fixed expenses are relatively steady, it's not so hard. You know what your housing payment is in terms of rent or mortgage, as well as cable and some other bills that you pay. Other payments, such as utilities, may fluctuate within a familiar range.

For example, if you live in the southwest US, you can expect your summer month's electric bill to be at least three times your winter's bill, especially if you have gas for heat. Except for those tough summer months, your electric bill is pretty close to your monthly average. You know that you need to save up for the summer, and you make accommodations.

You also know that prices tend to creep up a bit over time, which is known as inflation. The 21st Century hasn't yet seen the kind of big inflation scares that shook people in the previous decades, which doesn't mean it can't happen. Long-term inflation averages about 2-3 percent per year. Your $1,000 grocery bill will be about $1,020 a year from now, judging by that trend. With the dollar worth, well, $1, you can budget for these kinds of things.

That's not possible if the dollar has a huge trading range, as Bitcoin and other cryptocurrencies do. Bitcoin has been known to drop 32 percent in one day on bad news, but it can also increase by 300 percent or even 3,000 percent, depending on your time frame. If the US dollar was worth $0.68 one day and $300 the next, with no rhyme or reason, there's no way to accurately price something you want to sell.

Why (most) cryptocurrency is so volatile

You might be thinking that crypto is more like the stock market, because stock prices can drop dramatically on bad news. There is a significant difference between stocks and crypto, however. Crypto has no inherent value, but company stocks do. Stock shares are based on the business's operations, growth, and profitability. Even if a company is badly managed, there's some underlying value in the assets (such as machinery, equipment, capital, and reputation) that can be salvaged from it.

If the stock market suddenly decided that it was no longer interested in AAAA stock and everyone stopped trading it, the company could still operate and prosper for some period of time with its assets, people and clients. If everyone in the crypto world suddenly decided to stop trading a specific token, such as Bitcoin, it would fall off the face of the earth.

Cryptocurrencies that aren't pegged to an external source and allowed to float freely are subject to the laws of supply and demand. Bitcoin has a limited issuance as a policy, which prevents anyone from "printing" Bitcoin in an effort to devalue it for one reason or another. That results in a fixed supply.

Although the market for crypto and blockchain in general has grown significantly over the past few years, it's still a relatively small market. The law of large numbers states that as a sample size grows, the mean gets closer to the expected value and eventually converges as more trials are run.

One of the reasons that major currencies such as the British pound, euro and US dollar are so stable is that millions of people all over the world trade them many times a day. They're subject to the law of large numbers, but crypto trades are not because the market isn't big enough.

Smaller markets also mean that moves by big players, usually institutional, are magnified. In S&P 500 stocks (which are large and heavily traded), market moves even by a mutual fund company like Vanguard or Fidelity don't budge prices much. In crypto, however, if a big player decides they no longer have confidence in the currency and pulls out, there's a devastating effect on price. Not only for that particular currency, but for all digital currencies as well.

Investors, both institutional and otherwise, in the stock market rely on the long-term growth characteristic of stocks (typically 6-8 percent over inflation) to guide their activity. Speculators exist, but they're not the prime movers of the market as a whole.

They can, however, affect a single stock's price dramatically. In 2021, large institutional investors (mostly hedge funds) bet that the price of the stock of GameStop, a video game retailer, would drop because the company was expected to go out of business. Speculators, taking their cue from a thread on a social media marketing platform, began to buy the stock instead, causing the price to go up instead of down. (This is known as a *short squeeze,* because the hedge funds "shorted" the price of the stock to bet against it.)

As GameStock's price went up, the price became increasingly untethered to its fundamentals. In a large and liquid market, that condition is only temporary. It's pretty easy to pile everyone in at once, but piling out is a different animal altogether. Speculators who joined in the frenzy and got in late ended up being trampled at the end as the price decreased back to its true level.

The small and youthful characteristics of the crypto market also lend themselves to speculation. With no inherent value, cryptocurrencies experience a lot of volatility from news and even rumors. The hint of a new token in the air might send the existing currencies into a downward spiral for a time. By contrast, the news that a well-established company or investor is seriously considering crypto can send prices skyward.

Speculation only adds to volatility. As traders guess how crypto will move in the short term, their activity increases the price fluctuation.

In addition, some of the benefits of crypto add to its volatility. It's not regulated by most governments, which is a perk in many ways, but that also reduces some of the stability investors prefer for their long-term securities. It's still a new technology and many of the protocols haven't been hammered out yet, so there's a lot of volatility-inducing uncertainty still.

The crypto world, in many ways, is similar to the dot-com bubble of the late 1990s. At the time, not all entities on the World Wide Web (as it was known) used the ".com" nomenclature. Mostly that was reserved for businesses that sold things on the web, which at the time was an innovation. The dot-com market was small and relatively young. Sound familiar?

Warren Buffett, a legendary investor, avoided buying into the bubble. He said that the investment landscape was much like the car manufacturing landscape in the early 1900s: there were about 100 car makers in the US. At the end there were four. If you don't recall what happened to the dot-com bubble, it was followed by the dot-com bust when investors finally realized that 1800SockPuppets.com was not necessarily a viable business just because it ended in ".com."

On the other hand, decades later, some of the firms that survived the dot-com era ended up being titans of the current one. Google (now Alphabet) and Amazon, which in the '90s sold books only, are just two spectacular success stories. If you'd bought in at their initial public offerings (IPOs) and held onto the stock, you'd be pretty happy right now.

One of the reasons that the companies that survived did so well is that their market matured. They figured out how to be profitable, and created their own models for sustaining growth. DeFi and crypto are currently on a similar trajectory, as blockchain technology becomes more widespread.

Enter stablecoin

For a truly independent financial system to flourish, there has to be some pricing stability. Free-floating crypto doesn't cut it, but currencies that are pegged to an external, consistent reference can provide the reliability that a monetary model needs.

Many, though not all, stablecoins are backed by fiat currency, mostly the US dollar. Due to global concerns about the US dollar, coins may be backed by gold or some other collateral. Stablecoins can be bought on a platform, but by contributing the required collateral, a buyer can "mint" their own stablecoins as well.

They provide a safe haven for crypto traders, because many exchanges don't allow trading in fiat currencies, only in crypto. Having a stablecoin that's supposedly pegged at $1 USD gives some refuge during crypto bear markets (where prices are falling).

That's assuming the stablecoins remain reliable, which they don't always do. Relative to other cryptocurrencies such as Bitcoin, they're reasonably consistent. Compared to fiat currency, however, they're only approximately stable.

Another issue with stablecoins is that their owners and traders must believe that the reserves backing up the coin actually do exist. Surprisingly (or not, depending on your viewpoint), not all stablecoins have been able to pass an audit to prove they have the amount of collateral reserves that they claim.

As the market gets bigger and bigger and more stability comes from having more large players, it's likely that these issues will resolve themselves. There are several popular US dollar stablecoins on the market today, which you'll learn more about next.

Tether/USDT

This is one of the most well-known dollar-pegged stablecoins, and one of the first as well. It claims to be backed by a reserve of USD collateral that's held in a third-party location, which should keep its value steady at $1 per coin.

It struggled to prove that the reserve actually exists, however, because their auditor in 2019 suggested the reserves were only about 74 percent backed (MacKay, 2021).[1] Even so, it's the fifth-largest crypto by market cap. An independent audit in 2021 did confirm that Tether's reserves are at 100 percent. Not only that, but the state of New York sued the platform responsible for Tether (Hong Kong-based Bitfinex) as well as Tether, accusing Bitfinex of using Tether assets to get themselves out of financial trouble. The suit has been settled, with Tether admitting no wrongdoing and paying a fine.

Despite all the drama, Tether is easy and convenient to use and reasonably stable at $1 per coin. It's used frequently in Asian countries, especially China, which don't allow Bitcoin trading. As it's dollar pegged it offers a good exchange rate to yuan, and from there it can be used to obtain Bitcoin for buying off-shore.

It's possible that Hong Kong may find another stablecoin that it prefers, and the Chinese are developing their own crypto which could dethrone Tether. It's still popular for decentralized finance dapps, however, so only time will tell.

DAI

Rather than rely on physical reserves, DAI pegs itself to the US dollar by automatic execution of smart contracts and underlying crypto collateral. The contracts automatically execute themselves once DAI strays too far from its $1 price, so it's been pretty stable so far throughout its (short) history. It's traded on Ethereum and is designed by MakerDAO, which itself is a lending system on the blockchain.

When someone takes out a loan on MakerDAO, DAI is created for the borrowers who also pay the loan back in DAI. When paid back, the DAI is destroyed. Once DAI is produced, it's used as any other stablecoin and moves easily from Ethereum wallet to Ethereum wallet.

Any developer can use DAI as a building block in a dapp for financial systems that require stable currency. It's also used in a variety of smart contracts for other uses. For example, it's used in an interest-generating pool that allows the users to determine how to use that interest as it accrues.

It's even used on debit cards that convert it to fiat currency so users can spend it outside the crypto world (though this use is not available to US residents). You can see how valuable a stablecoin is for these types of applications. It's a big player in the DeFi world because of its stability and all the functionality that goes along with it.

USDC

This is probably the best-known stablecoin pegged to fiat currency (the US dollar). As of the writing of this book, there were 13.4 billion in digital circulation. USDC began as a joint partnership between two big players in the blockchain world, Circle (the crypto from Goldman Sachs) and Coinbase. It's backed by physical reserves (as Tether is) and governed by Centre, a consortium that sets standards for stablecoins.

Regulated institutions issue USDC, and those that hold $USD reserves must report on them monthly. USDC is an official Money Transmitter, which is a service that complies with federal laws regarding various aspects of money. In comparison to DAI, it's centralized like Tether.

As USDC is open source, a wide number of wallets and blockchains accept it. Communities exist so that developers can co-create and co-market new USDC dapps. Circle requires that you have a legitimate bank account in order to work with USDC.

Potential issues for stablecoins

Governments haven't figured out exactly how to regulate blockchain and crypto yet, but that doesn't mean they're not trying. The STABLE Act was introduced in the US Congress (and died there), which would require stablecoins to be regulated the same as banks. That means they would need similar physical reserves. That's a heavy lift for any stablecoin, but especially a decentralized one like DAI that relies on the blockchain to maintain its dollar peg.

The patchwork of regulations across countries paradoxically makes it more difficult for stablecoins to be used in more applications. A more uniform legal framework would make it much easier for stablecoins to enjoy wider use not only in DeFi, but in traditional finance as well.

Large companies such as Walmart and Facebook have investigated launching their own stablecoins. Facebook was ready to create a crypto based on a basket of fiat currencies including yen, euro, and pound in addition to the dollar. US regulators were concerned that the crypto would harm the value of the dollar and the launch was scrapped, potentially forever. For a variety of reasons (one being that it's currently not under such heavy scrutiny as the big tech firms), Walmart may be more successful.

Chapter Summary

Certain financial transactions require a monetary unit that is not subject to wild swings in valuation. A variety of stablecoins have been introduced, each attempting to peg the token's value to some external reference such as gold, US dollar, or euro.

- Crypto tends to be volatile by nature, especially given the relatively small size of the market and the youth of the technology itself.

- Stablecoins are the attempt to introduce currency that is stable so that it can be used in more financial applications.
- Tether is pegged to the dollar and backed by physical dollar collateral.
- Also pegged to the $USD, DAI relies on smart contracts and crypto reserves to maintain its value.
- USDC is tied to the dollar as well and backed by dollar reserves, but it's issued by regulated financial institutions and obeys US money laws.
- Having different legal guidelines around the world interferes with stablecoin's ability to grow in decentralized finance and elsewhere.

5

TRADING CASES: DECENTRALIZED EXCHANGES

Another intermediary in the traditional financial system is the exchange, where buyers and sellers trade among themselves. You may be most familiar with stock exchanges such as the well-known NYSE (New York Stock Exchange) or the LSE stock exchange in London. There are other commodity and futures exchanges, such as the Chicago Mercantile Exchange (CME or "the Merc").

These exchanges fulfill the role of trusted third party intermediary so that buyers and sellers who don't know each other can trust that the transaction will be carried out as specified. As you know by now, decentralized finance doesn't need intermediaries when there's the blockchain.

Buyers and sellers still need to find each other, so there are decentralized exchanges (DEXs) to facilitate trading. The users are able to complete their transactions with their wallets, and it's much less expensive than traditional stock trading. Why are DEXs so helpful?

Traditional stock exchanges

To explain why DEXes are so useful, it's good to know how the traditional exchanges operated. Over time the traditional exchanges themselves have become more automated and cheaper, and the digital exchanges continue on that tradition.

Stock exchanges go back to the 1600s in Amsterdam. The exchange trading floor you've seen in Hollywood movies is usually meant to represent the NYSE, which used a method known as "open outcry" before the advent of electronic trading. This type of exchange allows bids and offers in the open market, providing transparency.

That's why you see all those people screaming and waving their hands at each other. Open outcry, as you can imagine, gets very noisy so the traders use hand signals to communicate with each other. It allows the traders to read body language and other nonverbal signals, which can't be seen with electronic trading. It also helps them gauge volatility by the amount of activity going on in the "pit." For these reasons, a few systems still function on open outcry, including some futures exchanges.

The NYSE changed its format in 2007 to allow for electronic trading, notwithstanding all those Hollywood movies. Some stocks are still sold on the floor at auction, but trading is much quieter with so much of it electronic. With the auction method, each stock has its own specialist (market maker) that facilitates the trades and centralizes them. The traders in that stock gather around the post and commence trading.

Market makers are an important component of traditional exchanges. On the NYSE the market makers are specialists in individual stocks from member firms on the exchange; on NASDAQ (which is all electronic) the market makers are the member firms themselves. On NASDAQ, each stock has about 14 market makers, and they compete among each other for the best prices (Anderson, 2021).[1] Whatever exchange they're on, market makers help the trading flow smoothly by matching buyers and sellers. The buyer makes a bid for the price they want on the stock, and the seller asks for their price. The difference between the two is the bid-ask spread, which pays the market maker.

The role of a specialist on NYSE or other auction exchanges is more involved than that of a market maker on NASDAQ or all-electronic platforms, because they maintain an inventory of the stock they specialize in. If there aren't enough buyers, the specialist may reach out to previously active buyers. If demand is overwhelming, they provide the stock until prices stabilize. They buy and sell for their own inventories in order to maintain trading in the stock.

Once the trade is complete, the custodian enters the picture. Custodians are regulated entities (often banks) that hold customer securities and assets. They're the trusted third party that both buyers and sellers count on to move the money according to instructions. Other traditional financial organizations such as mutual fund managers, investment managers, private equity funds, etc., use custodians to hold their client assets.

Custodied assets are held separately from the bank's money. They're not allowed to be commingled or used by bank clients (unless those clients have a separate relationship with the custody arm). A custodian has three major responsibilities:

1. Trade processing: Tracking, reconciling, and settling the trade.
2. Asset safekeeping: Keeping records of ownership and valuation.
3. Asset servicing: Maintaining income, tracking corporate proxies and actions.

Trade processing isn't as simple as you might think. Now a *clearinghouse* (typically) gets involved. The process from trade execution to *settlement* (when the seller receives their money and the buyer receives their purchase) is known as *clearing*. The clearinghouse is owned by member firms, and retail investors need to have an account with a member firm of the clearinghouse. It's the member firms' responsibility to ensure that there are enough funds for the transaction and that the securities are available to transfer. All the transactions are recorded.

The clearinghouse nets out the purchases and sales for each member firm at the end of the day. The settlement date is the day that actual securities and money are exchanged, though of course all this is now done electronically. Different types of securities are now required to settle within a certain timeframe; for example, stock trades are settled in two days. You might see this written as T+2. That ensures that neither party drags its feet on its end of the transaction.

Seems like a lot of work, doesn't it? For one person or organization to buy some shares of a stock or whatever security they're purchasing? These systems all developed out of the need to introduce trust where none exists. The market maker smooths out the trading of a particular stock. A custodian holds the funds so that both buyer and seller are confident that the other will hold up their end of the transaction. The clearinghouse has a similar purpose as a miner, who checks that the buyer has enough crypto to carry out the transaction.

The system works quite well for its purpose of introducing trust. You can also see that it's time consuming and relatively expensive, with all of the intermediaries involved.

The member firms of the exchange take a cut, one way or another, for facilitating trades. They're also paid commission when they need to catalyze trading in the stock. The custodian needs to be paid for their trade processing, as do the clearinghouses. Your broker at the member firm must also be paid, typically through a commission. With the advent of electronic trading, prices have come down quite a bit. Even if it's just a small amount for each intermediary, everything adds up.

Digital exchanges

While the blockchain takes care of recording new ownership, checking transactions and providing transparency, individual crypto holders need to interact in order to trade. While there's no need for market makers, custodians, clearinghouses or even brokers in the digital trade world, exchanges themselves are still necessary for facilitating the trades. Crypto may move from digital wallet to digital wallet, but exchanges help them move. There are three types of digital exchanges.

1. Centralized

As you can guess, this is a little antithetical to the ethos of crypto and blockchain in general. They employ a third party (yes, another intermediary) to make sure the transactions flow smoothly.

These are the types of exchanges that make it possible to convert your crypto into fiat currency, or link your bank account to buy cryptocurrencies in the first place. The intermediary does make entering and exiting easier, and there are more centralized exchanges than there are decentralized ones.

Having the intermediary does introduce a "single point of failure." The entire system can be brought down if someone were to hack into the exchange.

Centralized exchanges also require that you deposit your coin, so you give up your private key to it while it's on the platform. They typically have an onboarding process that involves KYC (Know Your Customer) regulations, just as traditional banks do.

2. Decentralized

These exchanges are the ones that support DeFi. Without a central server or organization, there's no potential single point of failure. DEXs rely on blockchain technology to make sure that the transactions are processed correctly. Without an intermediary, trades may process faster and cost less compared to a centralized system.

Trades operate wallet to wallet and self-execute according to the smart contracts. The smaller altcoins are usually not found on centralized exchanges, so a DEX has more diversity of crypto available. The exchange isn't responsible for funds since it doesn't hold anything, so there are no KYC or other procedures.

Where there's potential reward, there's potential risk also. These exchanges don't make it simple to link your bank account to buy crypto, so you need to be a bit more tech savvy. Some don't allow fiat currency at all, which can make it trickier. If something goes wrong with the transaction, there's no one to call to make it right either.

3. Hybrid

Digital hybrids are designed to provide the convenience of a centralized exchange with the freedom and security of a decentralized one. Adoption for these is slow, but they might provide more benefits in the future.

Uniswap

This DEX is one of the more well-known exchanges, as it operates on the Ethereum platform. It's completely open source, so developers can take the code and create their own DEX with it. In addition, it allows users to list their tokens for free. (Centralized exchanges are profit-driven and require a fee for this.) It's the 4th largest DeFi platform (Leech, n.d.).[2]

It uses *automatic liquidity protocol* essentially to make markets for the crypto. Users pool their tokens together to create the "market" for all the trades in a specific currency on that platform. Automated algorithms calculate the price of the token. That way, a buyer or a seller doesn't have to wait for a counterparty (seller or buyer, respectively) to show up. As long as there's enough liquidity, or enough of the crypto for the request, the trade can be executed.

Uniswap charges a flat fee for each transaction and sets it aside in a liquidity reserve. When a user wants to exit the pool, they get a portion of the liquidity reserve equivalent to their contribution to the pool.

The price is calculated according to the ratio of the respective currencies in the pool. If there's enough of a specific crypto, the pool is large enough that additions and subtractions don't have much effect on the price. In other words, it's liquid. Otherwise the token will experience big price swings if a significant amount is put in by a *liquidity provider*, or taken back out.

Traders who perform arbitrage are an important component of Uniswap, because they keep the token prices relatively constant. For example, if the price on Dogecoin was higher on one platform compared to another, the trader could make a profit from buying the lower-priced coin and selling it on the higher-priced platform. They'll continue until the prices are the same, because at that point there's no profit incentive to continue the arbitrage.

dYdX

If you remember your calculus class, you might recognize that dYdX is a derivative. That's exactly what this exchange plans to bring to a DEX, not just the opportunity to swap coins, but to trade derivatives based on those coins. Currently it offers borrowing and lending, and the ability to buy on margin, or leverage your purchase. The cryptocurrencies traded on dYdX are Ether (ETH) and the two stablecoins you might recall from earlier, DAI and USDC.

Each currency has a pool that users deposit their crypto assets in, which makes them available for lending. That's done with smart contracts that execute themselves, so just as on Uniswap, there's no need to wait for a counterparty to appear.

The ability to trade on margin helps propel DeFi further into the financial space. Going long on margin means buying more of an asset than what you have on deposit, betting that the price will go up. Then you'll be able to make more of a profit than you would if you had only used what you had in your account. (Going short is betting that the price will go down, which is what the hedge funds were trying to do in the traditional finance system with GameStop, mentioned earlier.)

DYdX allows a user to trade up to 5 times, or 5X the amount they have. This is known as leverage. It's the same thing that allows you to buy a house with only 20 percent (or less) of the purchase price as a down payment.

Suppose you believe the price of ETH, now $100, will rise. You have $100 to buy 1 ETH, but you use 5X leverage to increase your buy to $500. (The loan will cost you some money, so you'd prefer the price to go up sooner rather than later!)

Now let's say the price rises to $150. If you'd just held your 1 ETH you'd have a profit of $50. But since you bought on margin, you have $250 profit instead (5*50), less interest and gas money.

Sounds great, but you know by now there's got to be a catch. Maybe you're wrong about the price of ETH, and it drops instead. If your collateralization (1 ETH) gets too low for the loan, your position will be liquidated and you'll also owe a 5 percent liquidation penalty.

DEX aggregators

DEXs may not be mainstream at the moment, especially given that they're unregulated and don't make it easy for people who don't know much about crypto and blockchain to get in on the ground floor. Another DEX issue is that they don't provide enough trading in some of the smaller cryptocurrencies for a liquid market. On the stock exchange, that's what market makers are for. In the digital world, it's hard to make a significant entry or exit on a DEX without a lot of transaction friction (which means higher costs).

Rather than introduce an intermediary to solve the problem, the decentralized finance solution is a DEX aggregator, also known as a liquid aggregator. They allow traders to access multiple DEXs for a type of crypto and find the platform with the right price. One dashboard provides all the exchanges that have the relevant crypto pairs (what the trader wants to buy and what they want to sell) so the right platform is easy to find.

Aggregators are so popular that even though they're a pretty new innovation, about one in five trades in 2020 was done through one (Lielacher, 2020).[3] By pooling all the exchanges together, you can find the availability you need. For example, suppose you want to swap some Ether for Dogecoin.[4] Ether is relatively liquid, but maybe you're looking to buy a lot of Dogecoin, like 100,000. There's no DEX that has 100,000 Dogecoin when you want to make the trade, but there's 20,000 each in five DEXs so you can make your trade. Or you find seven DEX that hold Dogecoin, but two of them have very high prices.

As a trader on a decentralized exchange, there's no requirement that you deposit your coin, so you keep the private key until you complete the swap. As long as you have a crypto wallet and an Internet connection, you can execute trades and you do so directly from your wallet.

Chapter Summary

Being able to exchange crypto is an important aspect of DeFi, and exchanges are now available. Decentralized exchanges stay true to the spirit of decentralized finance.

- Traditional stock and futures exchanges rely on intermediaries to produce trust at every level of a trade, which results in higher fees.
- Centralized digital exchanges have more fees and regulations than decentralized exchanges or DEXs.

- Uniswap is the 4th largest DeFi platform, and allows for trading in a variety of cryptocurrencies.
- DYdX allows margin trading in addition to lending and borrowing, which brings DeFi one step closer to being a reliable financial system.
- DEX aggregators provide the liquidity, especially for alternative coins, that a single DEX may not have the activity for.

6

DECENTRALIZED SAVINGS AND STAKING

W hen interest rates in the traditional world are close to zero, as they are as of the writing of this book, it's hard to generate any interest on traditional assets. If you've tried to open up a savings account to find that your interest rate is only 1 percent, or likely even less than that, how do you earn passive income? DeFi to the rescue, because there are ways that you can earn interest in one form or another on the blockchain.

There are two ways to earn interest with DeFi: one is to lend out your assets, which you'll learn more about in the next chapter. The second way is by staking, which can potentially bring in more than with lending but of course you can also lose a lot of money by doing so. With blockchains that use Proof-of-Stake instead of Proof-of-Work, those who participate in validating the transactions earn rewards in that particular coin.

Proof-of-Work (PoW)

This is the original consensus algorithm that Bitcoin created. It's used to prove transactions and add new blocks to the chain. As you might recall from earlier, miners compete with each other to validate and get rewarded for their work.

There are two main advantages for this kind of consensus algorithm:

1. Difficult to attack: The math puzzles that must be solved to add a block to the chain are hard enough that attackers need a huge amount of computing power and a lot of time. It's not impossible, but it's certainly more difficult than, say, hacking into a computer network at the one point where everything links together.
2. "Rich" miners are not in charge: It doesn't matter how much coin you have, when mining what matters is your computations.

There are a couple of disadvantages as well:

1. It's costly in different ways: As the chains grow longer, mining new blocks requires more and more raw computational power, not to mention actual electric power. Special software is needed to solve the problems as well. Now that mining is becoming increasingly more

expensive, it's also becoming more concentrated and centralized.

The software and the computations are useless for anything else. They can't be adapted for college math classes, or science data gathering. In other words, all of that power is used in only one way, which is probably not sustainable for the planet.

2. In theory, a 51 percent attack could close down the chain: When a user or user group takes over the majority of the mining operations (51 percent), they can mine all the blocks and take all the rewards by shutting out all the other miners. They can reverse transactions and create forks in the chain. Once that happens, the chain is compromised, and other users leave.

Proof-of-Stake (PoS)

An alternate algorithm, PoS was developed to address the issues of PoW. Miners can mine only the percentage of the coin they hold. For example, if a miner owns 5 percent of the available coins, then they're limited to mining 5 percent as well.

With this method, used on Ethereum and other networks, a miner would have to accumulate 51 percent of the currency, not 51 percent of the computing power. Someone who holds 51 percent of the crypto is less likely to instigate an attack against the crypto, because they would lose money as a result.

Validators for a block are randomly selected, depending on the amount they have staked.

Delegated Proof-of-Stake (DPoS)

Here's a democratic alternative to PoS invented by Daniel Larimer, a blockchain engineer who recognized that mining was too labor-intensive and too slow. He wanted a system that would be capable of 100,000 transactions per second, and PoW is too slow to accomplish that kind of speed (Crypto Stella, 2017).[1]

In DPoS, a fixed number of elected block producers (witnesses) add blocks to the chain in a round-robin type of selection order. Users vote for the witnesses, with their votes proportional to their stake, in a similar concept to PoS. Users can also choose to delegate their votes to another voter, who votes for them in the election.

Only the top witnesses are paid. There are plenty of backup witnesses since so many users are willing to take the duty. Though witnesses have a number of obligations, there's fierce competition to be one. Different platforms have varying numbers of elected witnesses; for example, Bitshare and Lisk have 101, while EOS and Steemit allow 21 witnesses.

All the competition puts some pressure on block producers to perform and make sure they're adding value. If a witness starts acting up or not adding enough value to the network, users stop voting for them, which removes them as witness. Since voting is ongoing, witnesses have constant incentive to take their duties seriously.

In addition to having elected witnesses and delegates, there are a couple of other differentiators compared to PoS. Block producers (witnesses) are the ones who create and sign new blocks. The block validators can be any user running a full node on the network. As a reminder, the block creators in PoS are referred to as validators, so the definition is different between the two.

A block is considered finalized and can't be reversed when it's finalized by 1 and $\frac{2}{3}$ of the producers. If that doesn't happen, the next finalization is the "longest chain" rule. The longest chain is the one that most of the nodes accept as validated, and is generally the one with the most work on it. (More blocks and more work makes it more difficult for hackers to attack.)

Because the number of witnesses is limited, DPoS can handle many more transactions and is more scalable than PoW and even PoS. The price of this additional speed, however, is the centralization of the platform. Cartels could crop up, where users agree to vote for particular witnesses with the expectation that they'll be rewarded by the block producer in some way, or other means of bribing voters.

While it's an excellent solution for apps that require high throughput, centralization means it's not as secure as one that's decentralized. DPoS platforms, therefore, aren't usable as a base network like Ethereum, where platforms are built on top of its blockchain. They make sense for high-speed apps as a second layer on top of a secure platform. EOS is probably the best-known DPoS network. Others include BitShares, Steem, Ark, and Lisk.

Staking

On a blockchain that operates with PoS, you stake your coins, which allows you to participate in validating transactions (as miners do in PoW networks). Either you lock them into your wallet, or subscribe to an exchange that allows staking. You then earn a set percentage of your stake as a reward.

This is a larger market than you might expect. As staking is older than DeFi itself, in 2020 there was ten times more crypto staked than the value locked in decentralized finance (Liu, 2020).[2] Although the rewards look much better than what can be earned through lending, they vary widely between different currencies.

Staking provides a higher yield than lending crypto for the same reason that high yield (junk) bonds do compared to regular corporate bonds: it's riskier. There are three main reasons why staking carries such high returns:

Coin price volatility

Except for stablecoins, as discussed earlier, most crypto fluctuates in price with their prices able to land anywhere in a huge range. Just like in the stock market or the housing market, the idea in the cryptocurrency market is to buy low and sell high.

Your staking reward could be paid to you at a time when the coin's price is high, and you'll be disappointed when it drops.

Payment in coin

If you've ever studied the stock market, you've probably heard people tell you not to put all your eggs in one basket. If all your savings is in one stock and the company goes out of business or into bankruptcy, you've just lost all your money.

If, on the other hand, you have a portfolio of 100 stocks (maybe through owning a mutual fund) and a company goes out of business, you may have lost some money, but not all of it. In theory you might not lose any money at all, depending on the weighting of the stocks in the portfolio and how well the others performed.

The rewards for staking a coin are paid in that coin, so you're adding eggs to your one basket. If the price seems to be on a downward spiral with no hope of recovering, you're probably not going to be overjoyed with having another of the same coin.

Coin inflation

As new coins are minted, the supply is diluted, which causes inflation. Just as inflation lowers your stock or housing market returns, it reduces your currency value as well.

If you want a more consistent return for your stakes, you'll need to look for crypto with less price fluctuation and larger market cap. Do these characteristics ring a bell? They might if you've made stock investments, because in the stock market those are typically the S&P 500 stocks.

You probably think that your less risky crypto will return a lower level of rewards and you're absolutely right. In the same way that small cap stocks, which tend to be more volatile, also often earn higher returns than S&P 500 stocks, your lower-risk crypto will return less than more volatile currencies as well.

Cold staking and staking pools

You can stake a coin by yourself, using just what's in your own online wallet, on a PoS blockchain. The downside is that in order to earn the most from your stake, you have to stay connected to the network 24/7. Has your power ever gone out in the summer, winter, during a severe storm, because squirrels chewed the wires from the connection box (true story), or beavers chewed through fiber optic cables to make their dam (also a true story)? Even a brief power outage severs your connection to the network and sends you back to square one. You may be limited in your stake's earning potential if you choose to do it this way.

Another method is known as *cold staking*. Rather than storing your coin in an online wallet that must be accessible 24/7, you can store it offline in a hardware wallet. The coins must stay in that offline wallet because if you move them to a different address, you'll lose the ability to earn rewards.

Or you could join a *stakepool*. This way, you're not running the connection on your own hardware or on a virtual private network (VPN). Stakepool operators have the hardware to stay connected, generally with a master node on the blockchain that is reserved for the network only.

By joining a staking pool, not only do you not have to be concerned about local outages, but the pool's larger stake size means it's more likely to write a block or vote on it to be added to the blockchain. That gives you more of a chance to earn rewards.

Staking Requirements

How much you can make by staking varies with a number of factors, including the size of the pool, the amount of coin that's locked, and the block's rewards. The longer you *hodl* (hold on for dear life, or stake), the higher your payout will usually be, depending, of course, on the value of the coin itself. The staking rules vary according to the blockchain and the coin, so you'll want to investigate them before you decide to stake.

You might also have to run a certain operating system or other technical requirements, because you are contributing to the security of the blockchain so there usually are some minimums in terms of speed and so forth.

For the staking itself, the coin will usually specify how many you need as a minimum as well. Not every network allows cold staking in an offline wallet; your alternatives would be either staying tethered to the network 24/7/365 or joining a staking pool (if available).

You'll need an online wallet (unless you're cold staking) that supports staking. The coins you buy will normally need to season for a couple of days in your wallet before they're available for you to stake.

ETH is one of the most popular staking coins as of this writing, since staking only became possible on the chain with the December 2020 release of the first phase of the Ethereum 2.0 launch. This phase created the Beacon chain, which is the PoS chain (the first version of Ethereum is PoW). Other coins include ZCoin, Tezos, and ICON among others.

Chapter Summary

Staking is a way to earn some passive income from your cryptocurrency.

- The first iteration of blockchain, including Bitcoin and the first version of Ethereum, used the Proof-of-Work (PoW) consensus with miners, which requires massive amounts of computational power and runs the risk that someone could take over the chain with 51 percent of the computing power.

- The Proof-of-Stake (PoS) consensus algorithm limits the network validators to the percentage of the currency that they own, reducing the 51 percent takeover possibility.

- Staking on a PoS network may earn greater rewards than from lending the coin, and is much less arduous than mining on a PoW network.

- Traditional staking requires a 24/7/365 connection to the network, but you can choose to cold stake (where available) through an offline wallet, or join a staking pool that gives you a better chance of earning rewards.

- In order to stake, you need a stakeable coin, a wallet that allows staking, a minimum amount of currency spending on which coin you choose, to satisfy a minimum technology requirement, and to let the coins mature for a couple of days before they can be staked.

7

BORROWING AND LENDING

I f you've ever taken out a loan, then you know that decentralized finance should be able to bring a lot of improvement to that process! Earlier in the book you learned about all the steps and people that are required to get a house mortgage, but many loans in the traditional finance world work the same way.

Suppose you own a small business and need a loan for whatever reason. Unfortunately, they don't let you just walk into the Small Business Administration and walk out with bags full of unmarked bills for you to disburse as you see fit. The SBA facilitates getting a loan, but it's still underwritten by a financial institution most of the time. You're just adding on another layer with the SBA, because they vet your business before finding an appropriate lender.

In other words, most of the time when you want a traditional loan for whatever reason, you'll need lots of documents that show you are who you say you are; the property or business (or whatever) is what you say it is; that you earn what you say you earn; and that the asset is worth what you say it is.

Even for collateralized loans like a mortgage, you still have to have reams of documentation. And you'll have to pay all the people involved, in one way or another. (The SBA is generally paid for with taxes, so at least you don't have to worry about shelling out separately for them.)

Prior to decentralized finance, what other alternatives did you have? Maybe Tony the loan shark from the hood who didn't ask for collateral, but who did have two goons with baseball bats as his collection agency. More recently, people who needed to borrow or wanted to earn money by lending began using peer to peer (p2p) platforms.

Peer to peer lending

Traditionally, men in dark suits sitting in formal money institutions like banks were the only recognized lenders. They had strict requirements, especially as smaller community banks began getting acquired by the behemoths. In the old days when everyone knew everyone in town, you probably went to school with the bank manager or both your kids were on the same softball team, so you could more easily get a loan.

As the bigger banks began taking over, they didn't have room for this kind of nuance in lending. Everyone had to obey the same rules, so the requirements were codified in ways that reduced risk for the bank and often made it more difficult for people to get the loans they wanted.

With the advances in technology, however, people began to create online platforms for borrowing and lending. The rates were often higher, because there was a higher risk that borrowers might default, or fail to pay back their loans. It seemed for a while that p2p platforms might actually dethrone traditional loans in personal finance.

Until, of course, the COVID-19 pandemic hit. Most of these platforms allow loans without collateral, so securing the assets for the investors is a massive problem when something like the pandemic hits, or potentially when there's another Great Recession or similar disruption. The biggest p2p network had to buy a bank in order to survive.

What's the solution for that? Many investors believe it lies on the blockchain in decentralized finance.

Crypto lending

The loan process with cryptocurrency is more similar to p2p lending than it is to traditional finance. There's the borrower, the lender, and the platform. Instead of a p2p platform, it's a crypto platform. It is, however, a bit different from p2p in that very often crypto collateral is required.

Lenders (investors) may get into the space to hold on for dear life (hodl) while they wait for the value of their coins to rise. Or, they may be investors looking to generate some passive income from their currency.

The investor (or lender) deposits fiat currency to the centralized platform. The borrower must deposit crypto assets to the platform, and receive a crypto loan. They pay the loan back to the platform with interest and get their crypto assets back. The platform then sends the fiat money with interest back to the investor. Lending platforms can be autonomous, decentralized, or centralized.

Most platforms ask for 150 percent collateral in the crypto, which is known in the finance world as *overcollateralized*. Should the borrower default, however, the collateral can then be sold to pay back the investor.

In addition to not having so many intermediaries, which makes the process cheaper, not having to go through underwriting makes getting a loan much faster as well. Credit score and income don't matter as much when there's collateral and no reputational risk to worry about. There are also no requirements handed down from a corporate office 2,000 miles (or more) away from where you live.

Nexo is a good example of a centralized platform. It started in 2018 and is licensed in the EU. Its users have to go through anti-money laundering and Know Your Customers processes just as they do in a traditional bank, but Nexo provides crypto-backed interest and loans. Some users, depending on jurisdiction, have access to a credit card based on their crypto holdings. Nexo has its own token as well, and users get certain perks when taking advantage of their products.

Advantages and disadvantages for both borrowers and lenders on crypto platforms

You've probably figured out what some of these are already, and as you know, there's no free lunch. Lending and borrowing both have tradeoffs.

Pros

Accessible for anyone across the globe

As with all decentralized finance, using crypto for finance eliminates the need for exchange rates, especially for the borrower. People who may not qualify for traditional loans due to low incomes, low credit scores or no credit history, or who have difficulty finding all the documents required by traditional lenders can borrow much more easily from a crypto platform. In general, all they need is an ID.

Fast approvals

While the loans may still require a review (depending on the lender and the platform), the approval may take as little as 24 hours. Traditional lenders can take weeks or even months to allow a loan application to grind through underwriting.

BORROWING AND LENDING | 89

Customize loan terms

When you apply for a loan at a big financial institution, you get their boilerplate loan terms. On a crypto platform, both borrower and lender can customize the terms of the contract to satisfy both parties.

Collateralization (for lender)

Should the borrower default, the platform will liquidate their collateral and pay the lender back. This is more secure than the p2p paradigm, where investors could lose their entire stake.

Cons

Crypto volatility

Unless the transaction is being conducted with stablecoin, the wild swings inherent to cryptocurrency can cause problems for both lender and borrower. The amount of coin that you have to deposit as a borrower could increase mightily tomorrow (or drop) according to its volatility.

As a lender, you might agree to loan money to someone whose collateral value drops tomorrow. In theory, the overcollateralization protects the lender from these drops, but 50 percent over may not insulate your entire investment.

Collateralization (for borrower)

If you have no assets, you can't borrow. Sometimes the traditional finance world will loan to someone with no collateral who does make good money and has great credit, which is not usually possible in crypto.

Platform security

Crypto theft is not unknown. In April 2021 a crypto exchange owner in Turkey fled with all the crypto assets on the exchange, and it's happened before as well. Centralized platforms allow the two parties to determine the terms of the loan, but the platform itself handles the transfer of funds and management of the loan itself. Decentralized platforms, on the other hand, remove the platform as intermediary.

Centralized vs. decentralized platforms

As you saw above in the centralized crypto lending where the platform handles and manages the transactions, there's still opportunity for hacking or losing customer money through bad loans or some other type of negligence. Also important to the idea of a new financial system, centralized networks require users to give up ownership of their coin.

Enter the decentralized platform where loans are made directly from one user to another. They work by the exchange of smart contracts. Users who want to lend their coins (often ETH or stablecoin) supply their tokens to a pool that runs on smart contracts, without giving up ownership of the tokens. In exchange, they receive other tokens that represent interest plus the amount of tokens supplied. They can be redeemed for (regular) tokens when the lender wants to get out of the pool.

Interest fluctuates given the amount of borrowers and lenders in a particular token, and is calculated for each block in the chain. Computing interest block by block means that interest rates can swing wildly due to the currently available ratio of lenders to borrowers in any block.

These platforms are also usually overcollateralized, and you might wonder why someone would pay interest on a loan if they had enough tokens already. Quite often a user has unexpected expenses arise, but doesn't want to get rid of their tokens to pay it. Or they're trying to avoid or delay the capital gains tax they'd pay on the sale of their coins. Sometimes they might be borrowing to increase their leverage, as discussed earlier in the book.

There are two major limits to the amount that any one user can borrow (beyond how much they physically have available in a token.) One is how much borrowing the market itself will bear. If a user owns thinly traded or altcoins, it could be hard for them to find enough borrowers to match their need. Actively traded platforms, as you might imagine, don't have this limitation.

The second limit is the *collateral factor* on the token itself. This measures the quality of the collateral. For example, on some platforms the collateral factor for ETH or the DAI stablecoin might be 75 percent. Up to 75 percent of the value of the supplied tokens can be used to borrow other coins.

In addition to the risks of smart contracts going awry, the variation in interest rates carries risk for users who aren't paying close enough attention to what's going on. Too high an interest rate could result in liquidating a user's collateral because they no longer have enough to satisfy the principal and interest requirements of the loan.

The three main DeFi platforms as of 2020 were Maker, Aave, and Compound. Together, they're worth nearly $10 billion, with $20.46 billion total locked in decentralized finance protocols (Takyar, n.d.).[1] Maker is sometimes known as MakerDAO because all the lending is carried out in DAI tokens. Users can bring in tokens such as ETH and generate loans in DAI. Aave and Compound are both open source, with Compound designed to host more financial applications as they become available in DeFi.

Decentralized platforms benefit from automatic fraud detection analytics, as well as machine learning to find optimum loan terms. The decision rules around approval make the loans transparent as well. The analytics that are available on DeFi also help lenders fine-tune their approvals quickly, using data from previous transactions.

Chapter Summary

Borrowing and lending is a key financial application that benefits from being located on the blockchain.

- Peer to peer or p2p lending was an important first step away from traditional finance, but they ran into trouble during the coronavirus epidemic and lost customer deposits when borrowers defaulted.
- Crypto lending is similar to p2p in opening up loans to a wider pool of borrowers, and in order to protect against losing money through defaults, requires borrowers to overcollateralize their loans.
- Both sides of a loan experience advantages and disadvantages on a crypto platform, and the price fluctuations of coins is one of the major downsides for lenders and borrowers.
- While centralized platforms manage the transactions, decentralized platforms use smart contracts to manage the transactions.

8

INSURANCE AND NFTS

E arlier in the book, we discussed the long and tedious process of obtaining a mortgage so you can buy a home. Another long and tedious process that's ripe for digital innovation is insurance. Applying for a term life insurance policy is bad enough, but try applying for a whole or universal life policy (which guarantees a payout at death, as long as you abide by the contract terms). The underwriting can take months and months. Being able to buy options By contrast, the world of collectibles isn't in dire need of streamlining, but NFTs (non-fungible tokens) have made them potentially more accessible.

How insurance works

Whether you're buying insurance for your home, life, or car, and whether you do it on the blockchain or through a traditional insurance institution, the principles remain pretty much the same. Insurance transfers the risk of loss from a person, household, or business onto the insurance company.

One person's house burning down would be catastrophic for them, and they would probably not be able to replace everything including the house just from savings. Instead, they pay an annual premium for their homeowner's insurance policy to the insurance company that holds the policy. The cost of the premium is based on the likelihood that catastrophe will strike, given similar situations and circumstances.

Insurers create pools based on a variety of factors, depending on the type of insurance. For example, life insurers have higher premiums for smokers than they do for non-smokers in pretty much every category. Smokers tend to die earlier than non-smokers, and therefore it's more likely that any given smoker's policy will pay out, compared to a non-smoker. The higher premiums reflect the higher cost of insurance.

Please note that the insurance company is not betting on any one person in a particular pool to die! Or a specific person's house to burn down, or one drive to get in a serious car accident. They have a lot of data that they can use to determine what are the primary factors for paying out on the policy.

Because they have so much data, the law of large numbers applies. They can pretty reliably estimate, for example, how many non-smoking married women between the ages of 25 and 30 with household incomes of $100,000 or more living in a suburban area will die in any given year. Remember that when you have large numbers, the mean and the median converge. In other words, there won't be a lot of outliers, which in this case means deaths for this population.

The number of deaths in the population in the example above is pretty small. Especially compared to, say, nonsmoking married women in their late 50s with diabetes with household income of $100,000 living in the suburbs. Therefore, premiums for the first population should be a lot lower than premiums for the second.

It's similar for property and casualty (P&C) insurance which covers homes, cars, etc. Who do you think would have a higher premium on car insurance: young unmarried men 18-25 or married men 35-40? Yes, it's the younger men, because they are statistically more likely to be in a car accident, so the insurance premiums will be higher. Similarly, living in a high-crime neighborhood is statistically more likely to result in higher claims on stolen or vandalized cars, so residents will pay a higher premium if their zip code is designated high-crime by the insurance agency.

Does that mean that all married men ages 35-40 are good, careful drivers? Or that younger men ages 18-25 are all terrible drivers who get in accidents all the time? Of course not. But the insurance companies base their decisions on the data that they have. If you're a young man aged 18-25 who's a good driver, you're being penalized by your bros. However, many insurance companies offer discounts for good drivers, which can lower your premiums even if you're in a relatively high-risk pool.

While P&C is often relatively easy to get, because the risk pools are a bit more standardized, life insurance can be difficult. Especially if you're older. Life insurance companies have actuaries that churn through the data to determine what the risk pools should be. People often fall into some categories that would seem to indicate a higher life expectancy, and others that put them in a lower category.

The insurance company wants to charge a premium that's not so high you'll go to a different company, but high enough that they can pay out the expected claims in any given year and still be profitable.

That's why the underwriting takes so long. Normally, unless it's a group policy, you need to take a health exam, including blood draws to look for specific conditions. Someone can appear to be healthy and still have high blood pressure, which is a sign of potential heart disease. If you're an insurance company, you don't want someone with high blood pressure in a low-risk pool, even if they're the perfect weight for their height and don't smoke or have other health factors.

They check for the warning signs of a number of conditions that are known to reduce life expectancy. A friend of mine, who was a cross-country runner in high school and continued to run long distances as an adult, had two strokes in his 30s and a heart attack at age 48. Heart disease runs in his family. Despite his other good health markers, no insurance company wants to insure him at a low premium!

Similar to taking out a home mortgage, there are intermediaries in insurance as well. The person who sells you the policy is not the same person who underwrites it, or determines which risk pool you fall into. There may be managers who have to sign off at various points in the process, contractors to pay (such as the health assistants who do your physical exam), etc.

DeFi insurance

By now, you can probably see some of the flaws of the traditional system when it comes to insurance. Number one, using computers for the data and generating these pools automatically should make the process go much faster, as well as determining which pool any particular applicant falls into. Plus, there are plenty of intermediaries to deal with, as you know if you've ever insured anything.

So far, however, insurance on the blockchain has not advanced far enough to cover many assets in the traditional finance world. Though some companies (such as Nexus Mutual) envision that happening and are working toward it. At the moment, insurance in the digital world is mostly limited to insurance on smart contracts and covering crypto.

In the US, you need to be licensed to run an insurance company. Though there's currently flight cancellations and delays insurance available, other coverages such as hurricane and crop failure have been developed but not yet licensed (McNamara, 2021).[1]

Smart contract "insurance" (in the US, only insurance companies are allowed to offer guarantees when it comes to finances) covers security and potential bugs in the contract's code. Members of the risk sharing pool on decentralized platforms decide which claims are valid, and their decisions are recorded on blockchain.

Decentralized insurance may also cover losses against tokens due to security hacks or bugs. You've probably heard about the crypto investor who lost access to millions of dollars locked up in his digital wallet because he forgot the password! You can buy insurance that covers a loss for your private keys (that unlock your wallet.)

In the US, up to $250,000 of your cash is insured by the FDIC. Since crypto isn't cash, it's not insured. Some of the exchanges are insured, however, and the cash you have on the exchange is insured. Other exchanges have created their own insurance fund for users, which in the case of Binance protects against a security breach of the site.

Option trading

In the traditional financial system, *derivatives* (based on underlying securities) can be used as a form of insurance in hedging the risk on a certain purchase or sale. They also, of course, can be used to speculate.

Two of the more familiar types of options that you might have heard of, at least when it comes to the stock market, are *puts* and *calls*. If you buy a put on a stock, you have the option of selling that stock. You'll pay a *premium* for the purchase. Therefore, buying puts on a security that you own will give you some insurance on your position in case the price drops.

Buying a call means that you have the option (but not the obligation) to buy the underlying security. Call buyers are rewarded if the stock price goes up, because they can buy at the *exercise* (also known as the *strike*) price, which should be lower than the stock's price in the market.

With puts and calls in the stock market, you can layer these together in a variety of ways to make money if the price range widens or tightens, make money without actually shelling out any cash upfront, protect a short position (in case the price goes back up), etc. You might have heard of collars, straddles, and spreads, and all of those are a combination of puts, calls, and the underlying security.

Note that if you sell a naked option (without a position in the security itself), you get the opposite results from buying one. For example, if you sell calls, you're rewarded when the stock price goes down; selling puts means you're happy when the price goes up. If you sell an option, then you receive the premium, instead of paying for it as you do when you buy one.

The premium for the cost of the options is similar to the premium you pay for an insurance policy. If the event doesn't happen that you're insuring for, then the policy or option doesn't pay out. For example, if you buy a term life insurance policy for 20 years, and your death doesn't occur within the term, you'll have paid your policies every year and eventually it will expire.

If you don't end up exercising your option, then it expires and is worth nothing. You'll have paid the premium and not received a payout. Whether in insurance or options, that's not necessarily a bad thing! You'd rather pay a premium every year and not die, or not get into a car accident that triggers the policy to pay out.

Similarly, suppose you sold a covered call (where you own the underlying security) in the event that the security's price dropped. If the price went up instead, you're happy that you didn't need to exercise your option because the value of your holdings is now higher.

When it comes to the mechanics of puts and calls, the market plays a part in pricing. If the security and/or its options are thinly traded, you're likely to find big spreads between the price people are willing to buy it and the price they're willing to sell it for.

Options normally have the number that you've bought, the month of expiration, and the exercise price on the underlying security. If you elect not to exercise your option to buy or sell the asset, then it expires on the date given. Typically you wouldn't exercise when your option is *out of the money*, where exercising doesn't give you the profit you wanted.

You'd exercise when your option is *in the money*, and it makes sense for you to buy or sell the asset at the strike price on your option. If your option is American-style, you can exercise it at any time prior to expiration, and if it's European-style it's only exercisable at expiration. Traditionally, then, you'd need to keep an eye on the price of the security to see when the price is right. At that point you would execute the option through your broker, and go through the settlement process.

As you can imagine, DeFi streamlines the option process and provides opportunities to buy and sell options on crypto. It's still a relatively small area of the market, but as many of the other aspects begin to grow, options probably will as well.

Currently, the platform Opyn allows option trading on a limited number of coins. Options are European-style (exercisable at expiration only), and settle in "cash." That way option holders don't have to put up the underlying token as collateral. The trade settles in the collateral, and the one who bought the option receives the difference between the strike price and the price of the coin at expiration.

It also allows for options that are in the money to exercise automatically. If you buy a put and the price drops below the strike price at expiration, for example, it's in the money and the smart contract will execute it.

As an example, suppose an options seller puts down 500 USDC as collateral to mint and sells a $500 ETH put option. You buy the put. If the price of ETH drops to $490 on expiration, it's in the money and will automatically be executed. 10 USDC goes to your wallet, and 490 remains in the seller's.

Collectibles

Other assets that are tangible and often need insurance, depending on the value, are known as *collectibles*. Art may be the best known category of collectibles in the traditional finance world, but others include antiques, stamps, coins, wine, first editions, etc. Some types of collectibles are more liquid, and investors have been known to enjoy decent returns when selling them.

In general, even the more liquid collectibles are relatively hard to price and sell. They're not recommended for investments unless you're truly interested in the subject of your collection. Prices vary widely, and a category of collectibles may pay out richly in one year and be utterly worthless the next (hello and goodbye, Beanie Babies).

Having said that, there are some categories that tend to do better than others, and items that provide a higher investment return than others. Items that are older, closer to mint condition, more rare, and more desired by other people are all factors determining how valuable the item is.

For many items, especially those that have historically been looted or taken from colonies of a prior empire, being able to trace ownership is very important. It also helps in detection of fraud, because if the previous owners of something like Shakespeare's First Folio are Joe Smith and John Smith, it's highly unlikely to be a true First Folio.

Here are some of the collectibles best known for their investment returns.

Stamps

They're small and lightweight, which makes them easier for investors to collect and store. Contrast that with wine, in which case you also need to invest in a temperature-controlled wine cellar. Best for you to drink it anyway!

Stamps are often released in small batches, which over time results in higher prices and they're easy to distinguish from one another or pick out from a catalog.

Toys

It's not always possible to know which toys are going to stand out over time. Though if you've dusted off a Star Wars figurine from the years of the first trilogy on film from your basement and checked out the price on an auction site, you know how valuable they can potentially be.

If you're collecting your toys or your kids' toys, they need to be in plastic coverings to keep them in mint condition or they're worth much less. You'll need about 20 years, at least, to let the market for toys work to your advantage.

Sneakers

Similarly, you're not going to find a whole lot of buyers for the sneakers you wore every day in the pandemic that are dirty and worn down. Regular sneakers, even if their straps, loops, uppers and soles are in mint condition, probably won't bring you much either.

Collectors are looking for the rarer ones and limited edition releases. Well-known brands are also preferred (Nike, Adidas, Air Jordan), not the shoes made by a non-name company that are the only ones that fit your wide, wide feet. I'm just saying.

Rare coins

As you probably expect, your penny dating to 1996 isn't particularly special. Coins that are no longer minted are more valuable. Most of the time you can ignore whatever's printed on its face, because it's far more (or far less) valuable.

Coins made with errors, and limited run commemorative coins are your best bets. You'll often need to hang onto them for a while, as you do with toys.

Some coins are made of gold or some other metal (bullion coins) and these aren't particularly collectible. The value is based on the price of the metal itself, and the government mints them in order to encourage investing in those metals.

Fine art

Paintings, sculptures, and photographs are popular. Living artists are selling quite well, but you can find older art as well that may be profitable. These pieces tend to be one-of-a-kind, which makes them harder to value. Ultimately, the value is based on what someone is willing to pay you, which is a tricky thing to determine.

Investors new to fine art should look to collect in newer categories instead of pricey items like Impressionist paintings. They're highly priced and not likely to appreciate much since they're already expensive.

Digital collectibles

Did you notice any trends in the discussion of the collectible assets above that tend to be profitable for investors? Things that are rare, or limited edition, tend to be more valuable. Collectors also need to consider storage for their items, especially in terms of space.

In some instances, you need to consider whether the category is already overvalued, or at least fairly valued, and therefore not likely to appreciate much. You may need to keep track of the ownership of the item as well, to ensure that you aren't dealing in fraud.

If you thought the collectibles section above was a lead-in to NFTs (non-fungible tokens) then you're absolutely right! NFTs address some of the issues discussed earlier with tangible assets. Non-fungible means that something is unique and can't be replaced with something else. A bitcoin can be replaced with another bitcoin and is therefore fungible, but Jack Dorsey's first tweet on the Twitter platform can't be replaced by another tweet.

NFTs keep ownership immutable on the blockchain, which makes tracing them potentially easy. They can be stored in on or offline digital wallets, so they don't have to take up a lot of physical space. If you're considering NFTs, you should consider whether they'll appreciate in price or whether they're already at fair value, or even overvalued. How can you tell? Well, like fine art, it's pretty hard!

Although NFTs started on Ethereum, other platforms are beginning to make them available as well. NFTs store additional information, which makes them different from cryptocurrency. Anything digital can be NFT (such as, say, a tweet) but more and more users are looking to use them for digital art, specifically. Some believe that NFTs may be the next frontier in art collecting, but instead of fine art, it's digital instead.

One of the issues with NFTs is that digital files can be copied over and over again. If a digital video is sold via NFT, people can still download the video from its video platform. If you're the NFT buyer, however, you are the sole owner of that art.

If you've been to college, think about all the posters and prints that people hang on their walls. Impressionism is pretty popular, so you've probably seen a lot of prints by Claude Monet. You've probably seen the same ones over and over again, as well. While anyone can hang a print, there's only one person (or entity) that can own the actual Monet painting that all the prints are based on.

For artists, NFTs can help them open up their market. Their art is now accessible to many people around the world, not just locals who might stop by the shop or the farmers market where the artist has a stall. NFTs have a feature (similar to royalties) where you can get paid any time the NFT changes hands. If your work becomes popular and your NFT is trading, you'll benefit from the action.

Buyers can support the artists they like with NFTs. You also get some usage rights, and bragging rights of ownership on the blockchain that are pretty much set in stone forever. Even if someone else eventually buys it from you, your ownership is still recorded on the chain. As a collector, you can speculate on NFTs and hope that their value increases over time.

Each NFT is a unique block on the blockchain, but they can also be more like trading cards where there are specific numbered copies of the art as well.

There haven't been a lot of NFTs linked to physical instead of digital assets, but that might change. Nike has patented a way to verify sneaker authenticity via NFTs, which it's calling CryptoKicks (Clark, 2021).[2] There are games that use NFTs, and in fact one of the first uses of NFTs was a game that bought and sold (virtual) kittens. (After all, we know that the primary function of the internet is to share cat pictures.)

Like physical art, NFTs of digital art are probably fragile as well. In the digital world, "bit rot" includes deterioration of image quality over time, the inability to open files in previous formats, websites going down or offline, etc. Not to mention that people forget the passwords to their wallets, and if not insured, that would be a problem!

Because NFTs operate on the energy-hungry blockchain, there are climate concerns. Some artists have decided against a release or drop after understanding the climate effects. Others have decided to be carbon neutral by investing in renewable energy. There are private blockchains, and some dedicated to NFTs that operate on PoS instead of PoW.

Another method would be to build a second layer on top of the existing PoW blockchain. Two users could agree to trade NFTs on their own channel, where the work would occur off-chain and avoid all the energy-intensive mining work. Once the users completed their business, the net effect of the transactions would be entered on the blockchain. Of course, clean energy itself powering the blockchain would also make a huge difference.

Chapter Summary

There are additional financial products currently available with DeFi, and more are expected as blockchain technology matures and is adopted by more institutions.

- Traditional insurance is both labor and time intensive.
- The opportunity exists for traditional policies to be on the blockchain, but at the moment most insurance policies are not generated from insurance companies and instead cover digital issues such as private keys to a wallet.
- Another example of a form of insurance is option trading, which is currently available for puts and calls on a limited number of cryptocurrencies.
- Collectibles are tangible assets, and a few categories are profitable for their owners.
- NFTs are primarily designed for digital art, and are the blockchain's answer to collectibles, at least for the time being.

9

CHALLENGES AND RISKS OF DEFI

In earlier chapters, we've discussed some of the risks and most of the benefits that are connected to decentralized finance. Now you'll get a closer look at some of the risks that DeFi and its investors face currently.

These may change and evolve over time, depending on how the sector moves into the future. (We'll talk about that in the next chapter!) Some of the problems are likely to solve themselves if DeFi gets off the ground that it's currently on but others don't have obvious answers.

Perception is reality

For many people, decentralized finance doesn't mean anything. They may have heard of cryptocurrencies in general, and they've probably heard of Bitcoin. Both these terms, however, have a bad reputation with a lot of ordinary people who don't know much about finance or technology.

The reputational problems begin with the original whitepaper published in 2008 that posited an alternative finance solution that avoided financial institutions. The name on the whitepaper is Satoshi Nakamoto, but to this day, it's unclear whether this is an actual person or a group of people. Which is unfortunate because creating peer-to-peer alternatives is a logical reaction to many of the events leading up to the Great Recession.

At first, one of the major communities for Bitcoin was Silk Road, a marketplace on the dark web that allowed trade in anything, whether or not the item was legal. One of the biggest trading markets was for drugs, both legal and not. Silk Road was seized by the US government in 2013, and that made a big splash in the media. The message was not that Bitcoin presented an alternative to traditional finance, but that crypto enabled bad guys to do things that were illegal.

A religious friend of mine told me that she would never use cryptocurrency because it was used for human sex trafficking. That may be true or not, and certainly plenty of traffickers use fiat currency anyway; she's not alone in believing that's what crypto is used for.

The Mt. Gox scandal didn't help either. The whole premise of bitcoin, the blockchain, and distributed ledgers is security, that no one can tinker with the blocks. Magic: The Gathering

Online eXchange, founded in 2010, began using Bitcoin as a currency.

In 2014, it was forced to file for bankruptcy. Users complained that they couldn't withdraw their coins, which turned out to be due to an attacker that had been draining accounts for years. This was not supposed to happen in the secure cryptocurrency world. Other thefts, such as the 2021 grab that occurred in Turkey, are also on the general public's radar.

Finally, even those who aren't attuned to the world of blockchain or crypto have seen the headlines when Bitcoin rose spectacularly in price, and also when it dropped just as spectacularly. Investors lost a lot of their risk tolerance in and around the Great Recession, so having something called currency that is wildly unstable doesn't give them a lot of confidence. (Yes, stablecoins exist, but they're not as well-known as Bitcoin.)

In order to be taken seriously and to become a true mechanism for an alternate financial system, more people have to adopt the blockchain for themselves and their businesses. Which means that DeFi has to shed crypto's bad reputation.

That may mean doing things differently in order to capture the public's trust. The NYSE hasn't endured any theft scandals lately; neither have other stock and futures exchanges. Although crypto was also intended to avoid central banks, the Federal Reserve, Bank of England, the European Central Bank and other major central banks across the globe have not suffered anything along the lines of Mt. Gox or Silk Road either.

While crypto currently is good for speculation, average people need to trust and feel relatively safe with the system they use for their money. Right now, the blockchain is not providing them with the sense of security they need.

Relative youth

Some of the issues with DeFi are due to the relative infancy of the idea. It was only conceived this century, and we're not very far into the 21st yet. Difficulties such as high price volatility are at least partly a result of the markets still being relatively small. As more people begin to adopt the system, some of that will subs;de.

It's a bit of a chicken-or-egg dilemma. People don't trust crypto because it fluctuates so much, but it fluctuates so much because not enough people are in the crypto market. These types of growing pains are typical for a lot of technology, especially this century.

It also means that the theory behind the blockchain is only now being practically tested, with the expected results that the original designers didn't consider. Although, in theory, the Mt. Gox theft should have been impossible, it wasn't.

Crypto designers didn't spend enough time considering the security of all the entities that touched Bitcoin. They assumed that the block security protocols and difficulty mining blocks would solve all the problems. They were wrong.

When it comes to money, most of the public wants to know it's safe when they put it somewhere. Having a lot of people lose a lot of value because the designers didn't consider security everywhere they needed to is not exactly a recipe for trust.

New tech always has bugs. People are likely to forgive growing pains when those pains happen to a piece of software, not when bugs affect the money that they need to live on. Major financial institutions, central banks, and exchanges spend a lot of money defending against attacks and implementing new security protocols to keep a Mt. Gox from happening to them.

That's a lesson DeFi must learn if it expects to be widely adopted. What are the potential failure points, and how do you protect against them?

Cars and dot-coms in the 20th Century

DeFi is young, and youthful marketplaces and concepts often drive speculative bubbles. People get caught up in FOMO (fear of missing out) and start investing once they see prices being driven higher and higher. (Which are almost always countered by a traumatic thud when prices come back down to earth. Gravity is real.)

It also leads to a lot of innovators trying to get in on the craze, without necessarily understanding what they're doing. New technology in particular seems to convince both inventors and investors that the new marketplace is totally new and revolutionary, and that the old paradigms no longer apply. However, human nature doesn't change. More on that in the next section.

Earlier in the book you read about Warren Buffett and his comparison of the early car marketplace in the US to the dot-com boom. There were 100 car manufacturers in the early 20th Century, and towards the end there were four. If you'd invested in one car manufacturer early on, you basically had a 1-in-25 chance of picking a winner. How would you have beaten those odds? Maybe you would have gotten lucky.

When dot-coms came around, the investors who were interested were older (typically Baby Boomers) and didn't really understand the internet. The inventors thought they knew everything, especially once the investors started throwing money at any web address that ended in dotcom. However, the laws of supply and demand don't change just because a new technology has entered the Thunderdome. And so the bubble ended in a predictable crash.

Even in the early 2000s, people set aside long-known investment truths to throw themselves into a frenzy. There is a lot of blame to go around for the Great Recession, everything from government policies to individual greed to corporate greed.

Once the floodgates opened, everyone could buy their own house that they couldn't afford in reality, thanks to forged documents and NINJA loans (no job, no income or assets) from questionable lenders and their suppliers.

The idea was that homeowners could buy a bigger house with a lower interest rate loan, paying the interest only, and then refinancing when the principal payments started. This presupposed that housing prices, which had recently begun to blow the roof, would keep going up. Which is not at all how finance works - no market continues to rise indefinitely - but people chose to ignore this inconvenient fact.

The banks got busy creating mortgage loan packages for their greedy investors - interest rates had fallen and investors were searching for yield. The banks didn't even know what they were doing, and very few, if any, of the officers responsible for creating these mortgage packages (known as CMOs and CDOs) understood the math.

The mortgage originators didn't care that their loans were unlikely to perform. They knew the banks would buy the worst mortgage and stuff it into a package and sell it to investors. That's decentralization (in a way) for you, and it ended very, very badly for the potential homeowners and all the people who lost jobs in the ensuing recession.

Currently, at least in crypto (as opposed to blockchain or DeFi), there are a bunch of people who don't know what they're doing and investors (and inventors) who have joined in the latest frenzy. After all, we are in a low interest rate environment, and holding coins can bring you more yield than what you'll find at a bank or in a bond. As the saying goes (usually attributed to Mark Twain), "History never repeats itself but it often rhymes."[1]

You'll note that cars continue to be driven, some dotcoms have become enormous enterprises that employ thousands of people, and people continue to take out mortgages. The question is whether DeFi is pre- or post-bubble. If it's pre-bubble, then it makes sense for investors and average people to wait until the market shakes out and separates the companies with a good chance of succeeding from those that don't.

Human nature and centralization

It may come as a surprise to many libertarians, but many of the rules and regulations around traditional finance were designed to prevent abuses and issues experienced in the past. They're not (usually) made up just to frustrate people.

Some people rail about the Federal Reserve and its power. It was chartered in the early 20th Century and originally designed to maintain full employment (which is not the same as 100 percent employment, by the way.) It only received inflation-fighting power after the oil crisis led to stagflation in the 1970s.

Licensing requirements for stockbrokers and insurance sellers are there to ensure that the people selling financial products have at least a tiny bit of familiarity with how the markets work and what's legal and what's not. That's because in the 1920s there were too many snake-oil salesmen selling phony stock certificates and other fraud schemes to credulous investors.

Selling snake oil with no compunction, making a buck off a credulous mark, and ignoring the consequences of your actions are fundamental to capitalism, especially in the United States. When the consequences are dangerous and/or life-threatening, however, the government arguably has a responsibility to address them.

For example, California's tighter emissions standards aren't because Californians hate cars. Los Angeles is completely surrounded and bisected by huge freeways, because it became a major city after cars became popular. LA's geography means smog from vehicle exhaust gets trapped over the city and its environs, especially on hot days. The state tightened emissions standards so Californians could breathe. Los Angeles County is one of the largest in the country in terms of population, so without the standards a lot of people would have needlessly died.

Note, however, that the tighter standards are due to government intervention. Conventional libertarian wisdom holds that the free market solves all problems, but that's prima facie wrong. The car manufacturers didn't voluntarily decide to make engines cleaner so people could breathe.

The tobacco industry knew that their product was poisonous and led to early death for decades, but they tried to squash the release of that information. The invisible hand of the market allowed them to continue to sicken and kill people, until the documents came to light. Even so, the government had to intervene by restricting tobacco advertising to children and taking other measures.

In other words, the 20th and 21st Centuries have shown that there are bad actors out there and that the free market doesn't always solve the problem, even though it should in theory. People want to have a place where they can go to complain or get their problems straightened out. Automated bots don't do it; people want to actually talk to someone to get their problem solved, especially when it comes to money.

Centralized exchanges and platforms have this capability. On the other hand, that goes against the ethos of decentralization in the first place! While centralization would no doubt appeal to many ordinary people who are concerned about not having anyone to turn to when something goes wrong, other users will want to ensure that the blockchain remains decentralized. If it doesn't catch on with the public, many of the current problems (such as lack of liquidity) will remain.

Competitive landscape: traditional system

You've seen how much a decentralized system with fewer intermediaries can potentially benefit people across the globe by giving them more access to capital without needing a sizable chunk of money to begin with.

The existing traditional players have a lot of power and they're closely linked with government structures as well. Any alternative that's going to be widely adopted has to be recognized as being just as secure as the existing structure, and DeFi currently is not.

You might think (or hope) that the failure of governments and banking institutions during the Great Recession might have an effect on people who use the current system. After all, only one (foreign) banker in the US went to jail, and none of the others did. In fact, some of the banks that played a big part in the meltdown are stronger than ever.

Depending on your political beliefs, there are easy scapegoats on the "other" side: conservatives blame greedy homeowners and the government for loosening lending standards. Liberals blame the mortgage companies who made bad loans and the banks who packaged the loans. The underlying structure, however, has largely escaped comment, at least among the general public and the media. Most people are not blaming the centralized system for being the culprit.

Not to mention that the existing system already has a lot of political power, in addition to money. Its members regularly lobby the government, and because of their deep pockets, they're the ones to listen to.

Can you buy, for example, Facebook's Libra coin? Recall that it was pulled due to concerns that it would affect the traditional system. If you're considering a cryptocurrency that's usable around the world it's not a bad idea to base it on a basket of currencies, not just the US dollar or euro or yuan.

That's not a terrible business model. Although you can certainly argue that an entity other than a social media company known for privacy invasion should launch it. It was pulled, not because it wouldn't succeed, but because it might succeed too well.

The blockchain will need to figure out a way to work around the power structure coziness to attract more business.

Competitive landscape: apps

There already is an arena that cuts down on intermediaries and costs, and uses automation to simplify financial transactions. It's known as *fintech*, which is the universe of financial apps that are available to many users around the globe.

There are apps to help people looking for insurance policies to compare and contrast policies from a variety of companies. You can get a term life insurance quote in seconds. You can deposit checks by taking pictures of them on your phone instead of hitting the teller or even the ATM. You can pay bills automatically from your checking account, or even your rewards credit card.

If you're a business owner, there are already automated payroll systems and HR departments. You can hire a CFO, COO, accountant, etc., on a consulting basis and pull up their bios immediately to see if you want to hire them.

From a user perspective, these companies are already regulated in most countries. There's no need to change to a widely fluctuating currency to take advantage of automation and machine learning to get a loan, for example. That means if something goes wrong you have a number to call, which the average person really wants in a service provider.

Human error (developers)

Tech works really well - when it's working! We've all been at a store when their connection goes down or their automated sales system stops working or had some issue with software, etc. Almost every software release goes out with bugs, because the prevailing culture is to just ship it and let the users tell you about the bugs. Again, people are often willing to deal with it when it comes to software but not necessarily when that software is dealing with their money.

There's no guarantee that a developer creating smart contracts can make sure they're bug-free. Things often get missed, even when you're working with open-source code or programs designed to be easily read, like Go programming language. Of course, there's no manager to call if the auto-execute feature doesn't work like it was supposed to.

For example, suppose that an investor buys an option contract on blockchain which is designed to automatically run if the option's in the money at expiration. A bug prevents the program from executing. The user on the other side of the trade might not mind, but that investor will. Who do they go to?

It's not the other side's fault that the 3rd party smart contract didn't work, so they're not going to make the investor whole. Who will? The developer? Will the investor even know who the developer is? Some platforms offer insurance, but what if the users decide they don't want to pay out that claim? That's the kind of uncertainty that investors are not willing to risk money on.

Human error (users)

In theory, pushing authority down the chain is the most democratic thing to do, and it (theoretically) makes sense for the end user to have more control over their financial tech. That's not always how it works best in practice, though!

Consider California's ballot initiatives. They were conceived as a way for the voter to register their personal preferences on issues that achieve a certain amount of signatures, rather than having the elected representatives make those decisions. Great idea, in theory.

Most people in the 21st Century are awash in information overload. The 2020 election included 26 ballot initiatives, many of them confusingly named. In some cases, if you supported

Cause X, you would actually have to vote against the ballot measure named Save Cause X.

Even if you read the voter information guide, it's a lot to wade through. Many people don't have or want to take the time to wade through it, and so they rely on sound bites or what their friends told them about it.

In a similar vein, there are still people (and not all of them over 65) who look frantically for the "any" key when they're on a tech support call. Giving them more authority over their tech choices might not actually help them make better decisions, as much as we'd like to think it would.

Poor user experiences

Most blockchain users currently are at least reasonably tech-savvy, and can figure out what they need to know or do when presented with an interface that isn't intuitive. Though they may still be annoyed when things are taking too long to wind their way onto a block, or the system is otherwise slow in processing something.

In order for more people to adopt the technology, it has to be friendlier to people who aren't tech savvy. You've probably heard the howls of outrage every time a social media platform changes the format of something its users like. Even if the GUI is simpler, it still takes time for the public to get used to it and get comfortable with it.

People won't use something that's too hard to navigate. If they have to wrap their heads not only around the idea of blockchain itself, and then figure out how to use a particular platform, they're going to give up and go back to the app or their bank where they know how to get things done. Blockchain developers need to take the next step of not just focusing on how to solve a particular problem, but to make it easy for people to get the answer.

Poor performance

Blockchain processing can take longer than similar processes in the traditional system, due to the large number of nodes that are involved. Centralized systems don't rely on tens or hundreds of computers scattered around the globe, and their transaction times are therefore usually much faster.

While some networks boast of their performance speeds of so many transactions (tx) per second, that's usually in a controlled environment with a much more limited number of nodes than what real-world users experience.

Higher transaction costs

Clients (or users) of DeFi do a lot of the computational work through decentralized systems. While the blockchain platforms are faster and lighter, it may take a user's computer some time to actually perform the calculations and get the digital signatures necessary for game or wallet transactions.

The more layers of cryptography (that secure the transactions), the longer it takes. From the user's perspective, it slows them down.

P2P networking

In essence, information on one transaction is sent twice: once from the user to the block producer, which may distribute it out to a group of peers. Then back to the user once confirmed, which may use a completely different set of peers to validate.

Because the paths are randomly distributed, they can't be optimized for performance the way transactions in the traditional system can. Their networks are designed and built for speed. While a decentralized system is safer from malicious participants and central points of failure, it can't guarantee any kind of data transfer performance.

This part of the process can also be very time-consuming on the blockchain, which many users will understand as bad performance from the system.

Consensus algorithm

Whether PoS or PoW algorithms are used, mining and voting take time. If the platform or network is having some kind of tech issue, there will be more delays.

The more participants on a blockchain, the slower it will be. The ability to scale up is something developers are currently working on. Ethereum's use of shards may help to solve this part of the problem and speed up the transfers, resulting in a better experience for the users.

Liquidity issues

As noted earlier, this is somewhat of a chicken-or-egg conundrum. Crypto markets tend to be illiquid because there aren't as many participants but of course people don't want to participate in a market with no liquidity!

Why is liquidity so important? It may not be an issue for early adopters, investors who already have plenty of liquid assets elsewhere, or speculators who don't mind taking on enormous amounts of risk. Many people (especially in the US) live paycheck to paycheck, and one of their biggest problems is the lack of cash in case of emergencies (Roberts, 2020).[2]

The general public wants to be able to access their money when they need it. If they lose their jobs, or the house needs an unexpected repair, or whatever the issue might be, they don't want their funds sitting in a market where they can't get to them. Or a market where one day their holdings are worth $5,000 and the next $500.

Paper (or digital) wealth is great to look at. If you can't transform your millions in crypto into a reasonable equivalent in fiat currency, crypto isn't actually worth very much. While stablecoins may be more liquid, you can't earn very much with them, at least compared to other kinds of coins.

Investors ask for higher rates of return for illiquid investments; after all, they're riskier. The cryptocurrency world needs some mechanism to reliably deliver the higher rates if the markets stay small, in order to compensate the investors for taking on an illiquid investment.

Sustainability

The fact is that the earth is getting warmer due to human activity. The Greenhouse Effect is due to the Earth's atmosphere trapping heat that would otherwise dissipate out into space. Certain gases that have increased due to human activity contribute to the effect, including methane, nitrous oxide (NO), and carbon dioxide (CO_2). Burning fossil fuels results in much more NO and CO_2, which makes the planet heat up faster. While three degrees warmer doesn't seem like it could do much damage, it would cause glaciers to melt and a number of coastal cities would disappear underwater, such as Osaka, Shanghai, Rio de Janeiro, and Miami (Holder et al, 2017).[3] Land that is now used to grow food will no longer support agriculture because the temperatures will be too hot. And so on.

Blockchains that use mining and PoW algorithms use a lot of power, much of which is generated by burning fossil fuels like oil and coal. That's not a sustainable practice, not to mention that many people who are concerned about the environment will refuse to use it. (Remember the artists who pulled back NFTs due to climate concerns.)

Fortunately, one solution is PoS consensus that doesn't require massive amounts of power to build and validate blocks. The general public will need to be educated about the difference, because if all they know is Bitcoin and mining, they'll be worried about blockchain's effect on the Earth.

Blockchain can actually be a force for good when it comes to the environment. Using it for the supply chain means less waste, and traceability means less fraud and fewer natural resources devoted to fraudulent transactions and products.

The networks, however, have to be PoS and not PoW. What happens to Bitcoin? It's not sustainable. The network has constrained the system to mine only 21 billion coins in total, and as of this writing slightly less than 19 million have been mined.

Due to the way Bitcoins are structured, it's not expected that the last one will be mined until 2140 (Phillips et al, 2021).[4] By then, unless things change significantly, the earth will be experiencing serious issues with warming as discussed above.

As long as DeFi remains on PoS networks, they won't be contributing to global warming. If Bitcoin doesn't change the way it runs, that might not matter. When catastrophe arrives, it doesn't really matter how we got there.

Chapter Summary

DeFi has the ability to provide resources to those in need of it, and to greatly reduce costs associated with finance. There are a number of challenges it needs to address in order to be a viable alternative.

- One of the biggest issues is that due to illiquidity, youthful markets, current developers, bad press and security problems, the general public isn't ready to trust that DeFi can be relied on.
- Creating a more democratic system also creates new problems, such as poorer performance and user issues and bad experiences.
- The structure of blockchain may cause performance issues, and the PoW consensus algorithm is not sustainable for the planet.

THE FUTURE OF FINANCE

No one, not even a billionaire or a mysterious crypto founder, knows what the future has in store. Technology doesn't move forward in a linear fashion, step by step, but by leaps and bounds. If you asked a Gen Xer (who would have been an adult living in the last century, but had grown up with some technology) when they graduated college if they could foresee what tech would like once they were about 50 years old, no one would have said they could deposit paper checks by snapping pictures with their smartphone through their bank's mobile web application. We had beepers and Palm Pilots in the 90s.

Some of the issues that decentralized finance faces now may very well be solved with technology or the passage of time may create some distance between the anarchy of the early crypto world. There may be some kind of significant event that suddenly brings DeFi and its benefits front and center to more people across the globe. As you've learned throughout the book, decentralized finance can be a great opportunity, but it has to become more widespread as a desired alternative to the traditional financial system.

The current landscape

In traditional finance systems, you'll sometimes hear people talking about TINA. That stands for *There Is No Alternative*. As of this writing, when it comes to US Treasuries (bills and bonds issued by the US government) and the US dollar as a means of exchange, frankly, we're in a TINA situation.

That could easily change, for a variety of reasons. When and how, and if it should for the betterment of the world, are arguments beyond the scope of this book. The important point as far as DeFi goes is that there's not much incentive at the moment for anyone not already using it to make the shift to decentralized finance.

The dollar works just fine, and will probably continue to do so for a while. For average consumers, especially those that are bombarded with information from the internet, their phones, the screen in the elevator bank, the screens at the gas pump, the TV or streaming services, plus books, magazines and whatever else washes up in the mailbox, there's already enough complexity.

Why add on more? Not to mention that what you know about DeFi, coming from those screens and services revolves around Bitcoin, thefts, and wildly fluctuating values. Why would you go from something that does what you need it to do (the dollar) to whatever that stuff is?

Many of the companies behind decentralized exchanges, some versions of cryptocurrencies and platforms don't have as much of a financial incentive to attract the masses as other financial products do. Most, if not all of the software, is open source, which means no one company can make money off IP (intellectual property) rights.

Also due to the decentralized nature of the business, the founders don't have the same exit strategies as other tech founders do. If someone develops an app in the traditional system, or some other kind of technology, most of the time they want to make it as big as they can to increase the selling price.

The giant tech companies pay a lot of money to gobble up smaller companies, and the more reach a particular piece of tech has, the more giant firms want it and will fight each other to pay it. Therefore, the original developer has a very clear incentive to make it easy to use and spread it to as many people as possible, even those that are not very tech savvy.

Giant firms are unlikely to pay to acquire open sourced tech that anyone can use and comes with no IP protection. DeFi founders and developers have little incentive (other than bragging rights) to build the network that more users want to be on, or the coin more people want to use. There's no reason for them to make their interfaces more user-friendly or the software less esoteric, because only tech-savvy people use it now.

Similarly, large financial institutions have no incentive to buy either. As shown by the Facebook Libra failure, they'd prefer just to shut the enterprise down than deal with a competitive system. At the moment, while some are exploring blockchain technology to automate some transactions, most of them are ignoring it instead.

What DeFi needs to be a true alternative

Essentially, DeFi needs to go *viral*: have all kinds of people from all walks of life talking about it, learning about it, and adopting it. It's going to take more than a cute animal meme or video to get DeFi going, though. Nyan Cat, beloved internet meme, sold as an NFT but that hasn't made blockchain go viral (Kuhn, 2021).[1]

Externalities that work in DeFi's favor could change the conversation. If the US dollar lost its primacy for whatever reason, shifting to a different way of handling currency would make more sense for more people. Suppose a traditional stock exchange or major financial institution got hit hard by hackers, not just bad algorithms as in the 2010 "flash crash" (Melin, 2016).[2] If actual cash money disappeared from the traditional system, people would definitely start thinking more about alternatives.

Otherwise, there are a few things that the decentralized finance world needs to put in place to become a system that more people use and trust.

Security

This is huge. Most people don't think about money in the same way that they think about other purchases, and they're much more security conscious about their funds. Being able to just take off with other people's money or cryptocurrencies (see Mt. Gox and others) has to be made impossible. I am not a programmer or developer myself, but it seems to me that this could be done with technology. The security of the blockchain is all well and good, but people need to know that their money is not subject to theft.

Until the average person believes that their money is just as safe sitting in an online (or offline) wallet as it is in a bank or in some type of investment, they will not adopt the technology.

Buggy code is another security issue. People are willing to put up with bugs when it comes to games that they play online, or in their document or spreadsheet, but it's another thing altogether when it comes to money. They must be satisfied that the smart contracts are close to bug-free and that they will execute exactly as specified when the conditions are met.

Volatility

You know that to some extent the high volatility in crypto markets is due to the markets being so small, because there aren't enough users for the law of large numbers to play out. Because there are so many alternatives with less price fluctuation, however, the market needs to solve this before they can expect many more players.

Scalability

Big, distributed networks move much slower than pathways that are specifically designed for a particular type of traffic. Crypto networks struggle at the moment when too many users threaten to overwhelm the system, or slow it to a crawl. That will not be acceptable to institutions and their investors, who are accustomed to lightning speeds on dedicated lines.

In theory, decentralization is more scalable. After all, you don't need to keep bringing in intermediaries or hiring people to take care of the additional business. Adding more nodes to the network or blockchain should not be a monumental undertaking.

In essence, the new version of Ethereum being rolled out includes more Ethereum chains, to help handle heavy traffic. That should alleviate the scalability problem, at least for a little while.

Remaining decentralized

Given what you see in the traditional financial system, it's not hard to envision pressure being put on various networks or exchanges to become more centralized. That makes them easier to regulate, provides users with a place to go should something go wrong, etc.

It's also not very hard to imagine that some people will want to skip the slow pathways of existing DeFi networks and be willing to pay for higher-speed access. That provides a way to make money for those who provide the access.

It also will end up concentrating wealth and power for those who can afford it. We've already seen it happen with high-frequency trading (HFT) on the NYSE, where traders try to use platforms that are geographically closer to New York to shave off a few nanoseconds. HF traders also invest in hollow-core fiber technology, which moves traffic faster than the fiber optic cables currently used (Osipovich, 2020).[3] They can afford it, and their transactions (which take place via algorithmic trading) can swoop in and eliminate opportunities for other investors.

Move away from early perceptions of crypto

The only players in the wild, wild west of crypto right now are the ones who can afford, or think they can afford, to take on the risk. It's more like Las Vegas than it is like New York or London, traditional centers of finance.

Crypto (and to some extent DeFi) is more of a gamble than an investment at the moment. But in Las Vegas, the house always wins. The whole point of decentralization is to remove "the house" from the playing field.

At least DeFi is growing well away from Silk Road and dark web infamy. It needs to continue in that direction to get more average people involved.

Keeping DeFi synonymous with crypto, especially Bitcoin, seems like the wrong move. The very word "crypto" tends to turn average people off. It probably needs to move beyond Bitcoin as well.

Bitcoin and all other PoW networks are not sustainable in our changing climate. The people who don't understand or accept the truth of global, human-driven climate change tend to be Americans. So while Bitcoin may thrive for a while in the US, other countries (and some Americans) will be looking for solutions that don't require as much fossil fuel or other energy usage.

Bitcoin's mining limit may make sense for people who are afraid of inflation, given that's the underlying reason for the total limit of coins. For people living in a world that hasn't seen much inflation for decades, or only in certain sectors or countries, there's no incentive to use it.

Potentially, inflation could make a big comeback. It is a problem in a few countries, mainly those who don't have strong financial structures already in place. For the nations with central banks and baked-in inflation-fighting mechanisms, protecting against inflation is not the key factor driving financial policy.

Some networks have started using the word *token* instead of coin, which is helpful because it further distances decentralized finance from its wild west, dark web origins.

What could happen in a DeFi world

If decentralized finance eventually comes into its own, given the current structures and platforms in place, then capital will be less concentrated into certain countries, regions, and cities as it is now. Inventors, thinkers, artists, and creators from all over the world will have access to money right where they are.

You might be wondering why that's such a good thing, especially if you're accustomed to thinking about money in terms of pie. If someone else gets a bigger slice, then you get a smaller slice. Why would anyone who's currently in a place with big slices want to change?

Well, money is not a zero-sum game, whatever you've been taught. It's not pie. More capital doesn't necessarily mean that people who are in developed countries and receiving plenty of capital now will get less. (Though probably some traditional financial institutions will.)

Having diversity in creation, ideas, and content makes the pie bigger, in effect. In other words, DeFi has the potential to unleash a significant worldwide Renaissance by providing money to the unbanked and underbanked.

More capital to more problem solvers means more problems solved, opening up doors all over the globe. Not to mention that developed countries have been working on issues such as climate change in similar ways. It's entirely possible that moving capital to new areas that don't have the same dogma or ideas could create novel ways to deal with current struggles.

DeFi could influence other aspects of the economy besides finance. Most of it is built on open source computer code. The same lack of IP protection for decentralized financial networks could spread, bringing benefits to more than just the wealthy who can afford to subsidize IP rights.

More open source technology could even revolutionize Silicon Valley and its sister sites around the world. Instead of concentrating wealth in a handful of owners and companies, money could move more freely.

Untethering currency from nations or nation-states would provide a number of benefits. Citizens of countries (or unions) experiencing inflation would be able to buy their necessities in a more stable market.

Conversely, suppose a country's employment and overall financial situation dictate a low interest rate environment. Such as the one most developed nations are in now, with low yields on bonds and savings accounts. Instead, a DeFi token could provide a higher savings rate.

It would also allow countries to change how their own currencies behave. Instead of pegging to the dollar, or leaving it to float, they could peg to something in the decentralized arsenal. There would be more options, which might better suit them. Although there are a lot of cryptocurrencies right now, it's likely that there will be some mergers and consolidations in the industry once DeFi takes off - just as it happened in the car industry and on the internet in the 20th Century.

Presumably the future of DeFi is on Proof-of-Stake or Delegated Proof-of-Stake networks and not the energy inefficient Proof-of-Work ones. However, that doesn't mean there is no room for further efficiencies. Because the mass of transactions on a network slows it down, Ethereum plans to split off some chains so they'll work faster and give people the speed they're used to. There may be other solutions that make their way onto the playing field as well.

Having loans or insurance policies processed and approved more quickly means that borrowers can start their businesses sooner. People seeking loans or policies don't have to spend so much time gathering documents and arranging meetings between five people with completely different schedules. Rather than spending a half day on the phone trying to get what you need to protect your assets, a smart contract can be executed in a couple of days and maybe even in a day.

Another benefit to decentralizing when it comes to insurance is that the pools could become much larger. With many more people paying premiums for a policy, the price of that premium goes down.

Also, with the capacity of big data and machine learning, insurance companies can get even better at predicting the frequency of events given a certain population. This may also drive prices downward for many.

DeFi likely makes it easier for those charitably inclined to send money directly to the causes they support. Sometimes donors get hung up on whether an organization is truly serving its mission, and they hesitate to commit more money. Especially if the organization is small, and doesn't have the staff to produce reports and get on the charity rating sites' radar.

At the moment, very wealthy people in the US are able to set up donor-advised funds which allows them to dole out the money however they choose and still take their tax deduction. Decentralizing funds allows people without so much money in the bank to direct money any way they choose.

In fact, DeFi might even make tax payment easier. With all the transactions on the blockchain, pulling up records is a simple task. For business owners (who pay quarterly federal taxes), having a smart contract send the estimated payment to the IRS could make their lives a lot easier. Currently wealthy people underpay their taxes significantly (Eisinger et al, 2019).[4] More transparency could make that type of fraud more obvious, and fewer people would do so. When the wealthy pay their fair share of taxes, the money is redistributed for the common good (at least theoretically!).

Another potential use for decentralized finance is in investments. The traditional system works very well for companies (and commodities) that are already traded on an exchange. A decentralized one could create mutual fund-like pools of smaller companies, especially those from underbanked areas, for investors to make money. No risk, no reward, after all.

Decentralized finance is still in its relative infancy. It's entirely possible that in another five to ten years, more technology has enabled completely new ways of doing business. From what we know now, though, there is plenty of room for it to grow.

Opportunities to make money from DeFi right now

We're not quite to the decentralized utopia yet, as you know. The technology isn't as widespread as it needs to be for that to happen, and there are some problems that need solutions before the general public is ready. Yet there are still opportunities for you to profit from what currently exists.

Obviously, if you have the answer to one of these problems, you can probably get some funding to turn that into reality. As a non-technical person, or someone who has other things to do besides watch a crypto feed all day, you can still make money from it. Some require more effort on your part, but others just take a little set-up time at first.

Active

1. Arbitrage

One benefit to illiquid and relatively thin markets is that you have more opportunity for arbitrage than in a big market where the law of large numbers mostly eliminates it. In general, arbitrage refers to buying and selling the same asset in different marketplaces to make money from price differentials.

One way to make money is known as yield arbitrage, where you look at different loans or staked assets. The rates fluctuate widely and there's not a lot of competition to narrow the spreads (differences) between them.

The other method of profit is across the exchanges, to take advantage of price differentials for the currencies.

You'll need to do your due diligence on the asset you're working with and keep an eye on prices, so this strategy does require you to hang out in front of your computer watching the trades. They're short-lived, so if you don't make the trade when you see it, you might miss it.

Also, be aware that there are crypto bots that act in the same way as HFTs on the stock exchange, which may make arbitrage on a dex harder.

2. Options

If you think a particular token is likely to increase in value, or decrease, or a relatively short period of time, you can buy an option on it to profit from your belief.

While arbitrage doesn't require you to have an opinion on the asset (all you're doing is looking for mismatched prices or interest rates), option buying does. It's theoretically possible to construct an advanced strategy using puts and calls that will profit as long as the asset is moving, but that may be too expensive to pull off in an illiquid market.

Passive

1. Staking

You learned about staking in an earlier chapter. By locking (or staking) your tokens into a smart contract, you earn additional tokens as a reward. Just as with traditional finance systems, you may need to either stake for an extended period of time, or deposit a minimum amount in order to earn rewards.

2. Provide liquidity

In DeFi, LPs are liquidity providers. (An LP is something entirely different when it comes to traditional finance or law!) You contribute your tokens to a pool that enables swaps between your token and another, and earn interest (in the form of the token) for supplying your liquidity.

You're not guaranteed a profit this way, because if one of the tokens loses a significant amount of value, you'll lose value, too. You can get data from aggregators to help you decide which pools are more likely to be profitable.

Getting into a (relatively) more liquid pool with less volatile assets will also help you hedge the risk of loss.

3. Yield farming

Once you've become an LP, you can lock the tokens you received (as a reward for being an LP) into a yield farm. Basically you're earning interest on your interest.

You need to be careful about the yield farm you use, however, because some of them can be unscrupulous about stealing LP tokens. Use a platform that's been established for some time and has been externally audited.

4. Lending

As you know, in exchange for lending your tokens you can earn interest on them. Because loans are usually overcollateralized, you don't need to be as concerned about whether you'll get your money back, compared to p2p loans in the traditional system.

5. Buy and hold (or hodl)

Technically, this isn't a passive income stream as the options above are. If you choose to buy an asset whose price rises over time, you can sell it for a profit in the future. In the DeFi arena, this is more speculative, as opposed to an investment in a company, for example.

Will the Nyan cat NFT ultimately be more valuable than the NFT of the first Tweet? Who knows? But you may find a digital artist you like, and buy their NFTs, as art collectors do with paintings and sculptures. Or you may bet on a token to be left standing after the industry consolidates at some future point in time.

Chapter Summary

The future of decentralized finance could be very bright. A few issues still need to be ironed out for DeFi to become more widespread, but it has the potential to expand to greater things.

- The current landscape offers challenges for more widespread DeFi adoption because the traditional system works well enough for many people currently, and existing financial institutions don't want the competition.
- In order to become more widespread, DeFi needs to solve the issues that prevent average people from adopting it at this time: security, volatility, scalability, staying decentralized, and outgrowing crypto's origin as a way to pay for illegal functions.
- If DeFi can overcome those hurdles, it has the potential to bring millions if not billions more people

online to solve problems and work on next generation ideas.

- Although it's still in the process of maturing, decentralized finance can still be profitable both for more active investors and for those who want passive income.

FINAL WORDS

You've taken in a lot of information in the course of reading this book! Hopefully now you feel more confident in your understanding of decentralized finance as well as how you can make money from it today. DeFi has the potential to remake not only finance, but other fields that use the same technology in the future.

Like other fields, DeFi has a lot of its own jargon: blockchain, cryptocurrency, miners, blocks, and so on. Now that you know what all these words mean or are in reference to, you're able to read other articles about the subject and discuss them intelligently. While the DeFi world started off mostly as cryptocurrency (namely Bitcoin), it's taken off since then. Currently, it's already more than just an alternative currency, and it has a lot of future potential.

You learned how the blockchain works, and why it's so secure. Though some thefts have occurred due to other weaknesses in the system, it's very difficult to hack into the blockchain and change something. That kind of fraud is rare, which is one of the reasons DeFi is so popular.

The distributed ledger of blockchain and DeFi also provides more transparency and transactions are easier to trace through history. Though individuals are anonymous, where the money or transaction has gone also makes fraud detection easier.

The decentralized world operates without a lot of human intermediaries and makes use of computer algorithms in smart contracts. As a result, the cost for financial services on the blockchain is much lower, and can potentially bring in millions of users who can't afford the fees of the traditional system.

Decentralization also means that no country, nation, or other entity owns it. Cryptocurrencies are truly global, and not tied to specific nations or economic policies. This makes a great inflation hedge for the regions that need it.

Decentralized finance is also more customizable than traditional, because users can arrange the interfaces to better reflect what they need, instead of what a large institution wants to provide. Open source code for the blockchain and smart contracts means that developers can create new apps based on existing code, and different networks can connect together.

You learned more about smart contracts, which execute automatically once the conditions are met. This allows for fewer intermediaries as well as lower costs. The backbone for DeFi is on the Ethereum blockchain, which pioneered the use of smart contracts.

In 2021, version 2 of Ethereum is being rolled out in phases, with one phase being the introduction of the energy efficient consensus algorithm using Proof-of-Stake instead of the previous, electricity hungry Proof-of-Work that Bitcoin maintains. Other improvements include splitting up the chain so the network isn't overwhelmed with too many transactions at once.

One of the issues with blockchain that needs to be addressed for DeFi to become more widespread is the volatility of cryptocurrencies. Because many of the markets are thinly traded, entrances and exits have a disproportionate impact on prices. As does the rumor mill.

To counteract the problem, DeFi has introduced stablecoins which are intended to be worth about $1 USD. In order to keep the price stable, some coins have actual physical reserves of $USD, and others are using algorithms to keep the price in a narrow range around $1.

Decentralized exchanges (Dexs) have appeared as well, to help facilitate trades without an actual intermediary. There are some centralized exchanges as well, but the platform takes possession of the token and handles the deal.

With a Dex, everything is executed with smart contracts and the user retains ownership of their token until it's actually sold. Currently the options on Dexs are limited (mostly to puts and calls on certain tokens), but eventually they'll be able to support more derivatives as well.

Token owners can generate a passive income from "staking" their tokens on a platform and earning rewards in the form of tokens for doing so. The tokens become a part of liquidity pools that users trade with, without having to wait for a partner on the other side of the trade to show up.

Users can also generate some passive income through loaning their tokens out, though usually there's less return than with staking. Loans are overcollateralized so that if the borrower defaults, the lender still gets their tokens back. Being able to borrow money on the blockchain means faster approvals and fewer fees for the borrowers.

Currently, some platforms offer insurance, mainly in the event that you lose your keys to your digital wallet or against hackers. In the US, insurers are heavily regulated, so there are few insurance companies offering things like life insurance or property and casualty right now. Just as decentralizing loans makes the process cheaper and faster, DeFi could do the same for many types of insurance.

A more recent trend in DeFi is digital art, as represented by NFTs or non-fungible tokens. Though others can make copies of the art digitally, the owner of the NFT owns the original work. Fine art is a collectible that can be profitable, and NFTs are a way to transfer collectibility into the digital world.

Although prospects for a more decentralized financial system can be very rosy, there are some challenges that DeFi faces. In order to be considered a true alternative to the current system, it has to be less volatile. That's a bit of a chicken-or-egg dilemma, since small markets mean a lot of "vol" and simply having a bigger market would narrow the ranges.

There have been some well-publicized thefts of crypto, even in 2021, and the general public needs to feel that their money is reasonably safe from theft in order to move to a new system. Smart contracts are developed by humans, and therefore they'll be buggy. While people may accept bugs in their video games, they don't like it when it comes to their money.

Performance is currently an issue, because the transactions are distributed to nodes all over the world in a random order. Centralized systems have dedicated lines for transactions, which can make them move faster. As the number of users increases on a network, the slower it gets.

At this point in time, most users are reasonably tech-savvy and can customize the code for their use. The average user may have a bad experience, between a bad interface and a slow network. That reduces the chance for widespread adoption.

If DeFi is able to rise above these challenges, it can absolutely be a force for the greater good in the world, giving millions more people access to capital and technology. Even as it is right now, people can make money from it. Those who don't mind watching prices and screens might choose to arbitrage between networks, because interest rates are not competitive.

Others who want passive income can loan out their tokens, stake them, and earn money even on staked tokens. Those who believe the price will go up may opt to buy and hold, or hodl - hold on for dear life.

Now that you're equipped with the fundamentals from this book, you're ready to take on DeFi yourself and start investing! Or speculating, depending on what you want to do with your knowledge.

As I mentioned in the introduction, I want to get this information out to as many people as possible because I believe DeFi is a force that will be disrupting finance in the near future. If you enjoyed the book and found it helpful, please leave me a review. Thanks!

NOTES

INTRODUCTION

1. https://www.entrepreneur.com/article/360815

1. DEMYSTIFYING DECENTRALIZED FINANCE

1. https://builtin.com/blockchain
2. https://www.nerdwallet.com/article/investing/cryptocurrency-7-things-to-know
3. https://www.theverge.com/2021/1/12/22227535/nyt-bitcoin-millions-forgot-passwords-digital-wallet

2. THE ADVANTAGES OF DEFI

1. https://medium.com/hbus-official/the-how-and-why-of-blockchain-transparency-b3f3465f6989
2. https://www.thebalance.com/what-is-a-peg-to-the-dollar-3305925

3. DECENTRALIZED INFRASTRUCTURE AND SMART CONTRACTS

1. https://corpgov.law.harvard.edu/2018/05/26/an-introduction-to-smart-contracts-and-their-potential-and-inherent-limitations/

4. DECENTRALIZED (STABLE) MONEY

1. https://www.valuethemarkets.com/2021/04/13/tether-usdt-stablecoin-crush-bitcoin/

5. TRADING CASES: DECENTRALIZED EXCHANGES

1. https://www.investopedia.com/ask/answers/128.asp
2. https://www.coindesk.com/what-is-uniswap-complete-guide
3. https://trustwallet.com/blog/the-role-of-dex-aggregators
4. Please note this is an example only, not a suggestion!

6. DECENTRALIZED SAVINGS AND STAKING

1. https://hackernoon.com/explain-delegated-proof-of-stake-like-im-5-888b2a74897d
2. https://www.okex.com/academy/en/passive-earnings-in-crypto-defi-lending-and-staking-in-a-zero-interest-economy

7. BORROWING AND LENDING

1. https://www.leewayhertz.com/how-defi-lending-works/

8. INSURANCE AND NFTS

1. https://www.benzinga.com/money/best-crypto-and-defi-insurance/
2. https://www.theverge.com/22310188/nft-explainer-what-is-blockchain-crypto-art-faq

9. CHALLENGES AND RISKS OF DEFI

1. https://quoteinvestigator.com/2014/01/12/history-rhymes/
2. https://seekingalpha.com/article/4363924-safety-liquidity-return-why-cash-is-important-hedge
3. https://www.theguardian.com/cities/ng-interactive/2017/nov/03/three-degree-world-cities-drowned-global-warming
4. https://decrypt.co/33124/what-will-happen-to-bitcoin-after-all-21-million-are-mined

10. THE FUTURE OF FINANCE

1. https://www.coindesk.com/nyan-cat-nft-ethereum-meme
2. https://www.businessinsider.com/what-actually-caused-2010-flash-crash-2016-1
3. https://www.wsj.com/articles/high-frequency-traders-push-closer-to-light-speed-with-cutting-edge-cables-11608028200
4. https://www.propublica.org/article/ultrawealthy-taxes-irs-internal-revenue-service-global-high-wealth-audits

Made in the USA
Monee, IL
02 August 2021

74815761R00095